NATURAL
DISASTERS

Investigate Earth's Most Destructive Forces

with **25** PROJECTS

Kathleen M. Reilly

Illustrated by Tom Casteel

~ Titles in the *Build It Yourself* Series ~

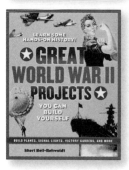

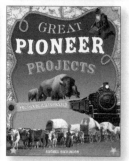
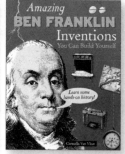

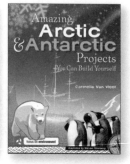

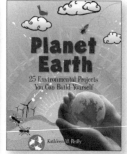

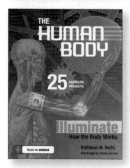
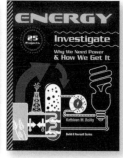

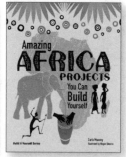

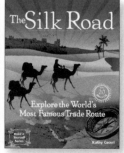
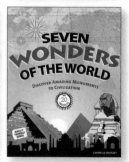

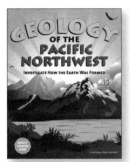

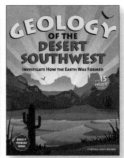

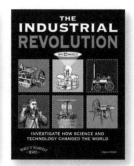

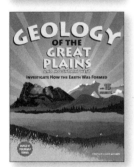

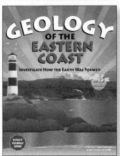

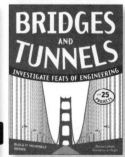

ALSO AVAILABLE IN
Spanish/Español

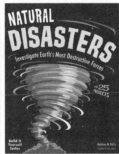

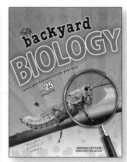

ALSO AVAILABLE IN
Spanish/Español

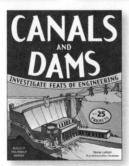

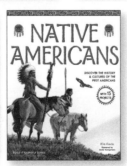

Nomad Press is committed to preserving ancient forests and natural resources. We elected to print *Natural Disasters: Investigate Earth's Most Destructive Forces* on 4,007 lbs. of Williamsburg Recycled 30% offset.

Nomad Press made this paper choice because our printer, Sheridan Books, is a member of Green Press Initiative, a nonprofit program dedicated to supporting authors, publishers, and suppliers in their efforts to reduce their use of fiber obtained from endangered forests.

For more information, visit **www.greenpressinitiative.org**.

Nomad Press
A division of Nomad Communications
10 9 8 7 6 5 4 3 2 1

This book was manufactured by Sheridan Books,
Ann Arbor, MI USA.
December 2012, Job #342264
ISBN: 978-1-61930-147-4

Illustrations by Tom Casteel
Educational Consultant, Marla Conn

Questions regarding the ordering of this book should be addressed to
Independent Publishers Group
814 N. Franklin St.
Chicago, IL 60610
www.ipgbook.com

Nomad Press
2456 Christian St.
White River Junction, VT 05001
www.nomadpress.net

CONTENTS

TIMELINE

79 CE Mount Vesuvius erupts, burying the Italian town of Pompeii.

1783 Laki erupts in Iceland over a period of eight months. It was the second-greatest volcanic eruption of the past 1,000 years.

1815 Mt. Tambora in Indonesia erupts in the most powerful volcanic event in recorded history. So much ash enters the atmosphere that people in Europe and North America call it the Year without a Summer.

1871 The deadliest fire in United States history burns in the forests of Wisconsin, claiming 2,500 lives. On the same day, the Great Chicago Fire destroys the city and killed hundreds of people.

1883 Krakatau erupts in Indonesia, affecting weather and temperature patterns around the world for years.

1888 One of the most severe blizzards in recorded history hits the East Coast of the United States.

1889 The deadliest flash flood in history claims 2,000 lives when a dam breaks near Johnstown, Pennsylvania.

1906 The city of San Francisco is destroyed by an earthquake that kills thousands of people.

1908 A meteoroid or piece of a comet explodes above western Siberia in Russia, toppling 80 million trees. Called the Tunguska event, the explosion packed more energy than an atomic bomb.

1910 The worst avalanche in United States history hits Wellington, Washington.

1910 The Great Fire of 1910 in Washington, Idaho, and Montana burns an area the size of the state of Connecticut.

1912 Novarupta volcano erupts in Alaska, the largest eruption of the twentieth century.

1930s Charles Richter develops the Richter scale to measure the intensity of earthquakes.

1930s A long drought in southern areas of the Great Plains is so severe that the area is called the Dust Bowl.

TIMELINE

1931 In the deadliest natural disaster in history, central China floods claim between 2,500,000 and 3,700,000 lives.

1958 A mega tsunami, 1,720 feet high (524 meters), is created in Lituya Bay, Alaska, when an earthquake splits 90 million tons of rock and ice off the side of a mountain, which falls into the bay like a cannonball.

1960 The strongest earthquake ever recorded, measuring 9.5 on the Richter scale, occurs in Chile.

1972 The deadliest blizzard in history batters Iran, claiming 4,000 lives.

1980 Mount St. Helens in Washington blows its top off, killing 57 people.

1984 The first recorded limnic eruption, at Lake Monoun in Cameroon, kills 37 people.

1986 The second recorded limnic eruption, at Lake Nyos in Cameroon, kills more than 1,700 people.

1991 Mount Pinatubo erupts in the Philippines, the second-largest volcanic eruption in the twentieth century.

2004 An earthquake off the coast of Sumatra, the third-largest ever recorded, at 9.1, launches the deadliest tsunami ever recorded. It kills 230,000 people in countries bordering the Indian Ocean.

2005 Hurricane Katrina hits southeastern Louisiana and floods New Orleans.

2011 A 9.0 earthquake off the coast of Japan creates a 133-foot tsunami that destroys cities and damages several nuclear power plants.

2011 The largest tornado outbreak is recorded with over 300 tornadoes in the eastern half of the United States.

2011 The town of Joplin, Missouri, is destroyed by a multiple vortex tornado over a mile wide.

2011 A magnitude 5.8 earthquake occurs in Virginia, the largest earthquake on the East Coast since 1897.

2011 Tropical Storm Irene dumps such heavy rain on New York and Vermont that heavy flooding destroys roads and bridges.

INTRODUCTION
WHAT ARE NATURAL DISASTERS?

Our planet is perfectly suited for life. It's the ideal distance from the sun so it's not too hot and not too cold. It also has the right mix of water, **OXYGEN**, and other vital elements that support life. But there's more to Earth than that.

OXYGEN: a gas in the air that people and animals need to breathe to stay alive.

EARTHQUAKE: when pieces of the outer layer of the earth suddenly move.

ERUPT: to burst suddenly.

VOLCANO: an opening in the earth's surface through which lava, ash, and gases can burst out.

ATMOSPHERE: the gases surrounding the earth.

WATER VAPOR: the gas form of water in the air.

Deep inside the earth, melted rock flows like Silly Putty. That's just how our planet is made. But sometimes this can cause big problems like **EARTHQUAKES** and **ERUPTING VOLCANOES**.

And above the earth, there is an **ATMOSPHERE** with **WATER VAPOR** and moving air. On normal days these are working together to make the weather patterns we're used to.

Usually a thunderstorm or heavy rain is no big deal. But sometimes the parts collide to create something bigger, like a hurricane or a tornado.

For all the progress and developments humans make over the years, we will never control the forces of nature. We can learn from natural disasters and develop better alert systems and stronger structures, or avoid living in places that are most at risk for a natural disaster. But it's all about learning to live with nature. And sometimes Mother Nature forces us to learn the hard way!

Imagine living in ancient times, at the base of a huge, smoking mountain. You and your family might believe the mountain is the home of a powerful spirit, and if you don't treat the mountain well, the spirit will get mad.

DID YOU KNOW?

A natural disaster is a sudden event that causes a lot of destruction, sometimes even death. Floods, storms, erupting volcanoes, and earthquakes are all natural disasters.

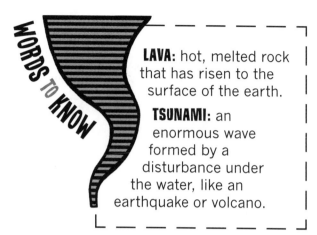

WORDS TO KNOW

LAVA: hot, melted rock that has risen to the surface of the earth.

TSUNAMI: an enormous wave formed by a disturbance under the water, like an earthquake or volcano.

Then one day, there's a rumble. Out of nowhere, the mountain suddenly begins belching smoke and ash into the sky! Fiery hot **LAVA** pours down the sides. You and your family flee your village along with everyone else. It is years before anyone can live in the area again.

FOR OUR ANCESTORS, NATURAL DISASTERS WERE MYSTERIES.

Your family might decide that the mountain spirit was angry and lashed out at your village. Why? Because in ancient times, people didn't really have any way of understanding the earth like we do today. They didn't know that the mountain was a volcano, and it was erupting because of hot, melted rock deep in the earth.

TODAY, EARTHQUAKES, TSUNAMIS, AND ERUPTING VOLCANOES ALL GRAB HEADLINES AROUND THE WORLD.

THE HERALD NEWS

VOL XXXI   PUBLICATION OF VALLEY CORP.   45 PAGES   75¢

TORNADO RAVAGES CITY

SURVIVORS DIGGING OUT

THOUSANDS HOMELESS

Hot lava, broken ground, powerful waves, and swirling winds. It's like the earth has completely gone wild when things like this happen. Nothing is peaceful and calm. When nature gets out of control, people, creatures, and the environment are all impacted.

In this book, you'll learn all about natural disasters. You'll find out what causes them, what their impact on ancient **CIVILIZATIONS** has been, and how people today cope with natural disasters. And you'll see how scientists are working to find ways to predict what's going to happen so people have enough warning to prevent tragedies.

Have you ever experienced a natural disaster? Then you know how upsetting it can be. But if you understand how to plan ahead and stay safe, you can help yourself and the people you care about.

WORDS TO KNOW

CIVILIZATION: a community of people that is advanced in art, science, and government.

DID YOU KNOW?

The moon has earthquakes, too. They're much smaller and less frequent than on Earth, and they're called moonquakes!

EARTHQUAKE SAFETY

Fortunately, the chances of being in a big earthquake are fairly low. But there are things you can do to protect yourself, your family, and your friends during an earthquake. If you're outside, try to get to a place that's in the open and away from anything that can fall on you. If you're inside, get under something protective, like a sturdy table, or stand under a door frame where the structure will be stronger. If you live in an area that's prone to earthquakes, be sure to make an emergency earthquake box. Add things like water, canned food, flashlights, and batteries, so if you lose power, you can take care of yourselves for a while. ◉

CHAPTER ONE
EARTHQUAKES AND TSUNAMIS

In the afternoon of August 23, 2011, people all along the northeastern coast of the United States were startled when they suddenly began to feel the ground move and roll underneath them. In Mineral Springs, Virginia, some buildings cracked and pieces fell off!

WORDS TO KNOW

MAGNITUDE: the measurement of the strength of an earthquake.

INNER CORE: the very middle of the earth.

OUTER CORE: the layer of the earth between the inner core and the mantle.

MOLTEN: melted by heat to form a liquid.

MANTLE: the layer of the earth around the core.

DENSE: tightly packed together.

For a few minutes, people from Canada to North Carolina were confused and even a little panicked. What was happening? It was a rare East Coast earthquake—and it was a big one. The earthquake had a **MAGNITUDE** of 5.8, which is a pretty hefty quake.

While other parts of the world are used to earthquakes, this was a big surprise for people who had never experienced one before. The last time an earthquake that large hit the East Coast was in 1897.

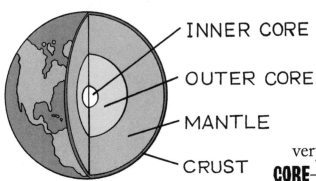

INNER CORE

OUTER CORE

MANTLE

CRUST

WHAT'S SHAKING?

Why do earthquakes happen? Because of the structure of the earth. Our planet isn't just a solid rock. Scientists believe the very center of the earth—the **INNER CORE**—is made of solid metal about as hot as the surface of the sun. The inner core is just a little smaller than the moon. Surrounding the inner core is the **OUTER CORE**. That's made of **MOLTEN** metal, but not as hot. Next is the **MANTLE**, the thickest part of the earth. The mantle is made of rock that is still hot enough to be partially melted. The mantle closest to the core is the hottest and most **DENSE**, while the mantle farther away is cooler.

CRUST: the outer surface of the earth.

PLATES: large sections of the earth's crust.

The mantle is a lot like hot pavement that's being poured to make a road. It's thick but still fluid enough to move. Surrounding the mantle is the final layer of the earth, called the **CRUST**. The crust is the only hard layer. But compared to the rest of the earth, the crust is pretty thin—like the skin of a peach is to the rest of the fruit. The crust is broken up into pieces that fit together like a puzzle, called **PLATES**. Because the plates are on the mantle that flows, the plates bump in some places. This is where earthquakes happen.

PACIFIC RING OF FIRE

Almost 90 percent of the earth's earthquakes happen in one area. Right around the Pacific Ocean there are several plates all rubbing against each other. There are so many earthquakes and volcanoes there that it's called the Pacific Ring of Fire.

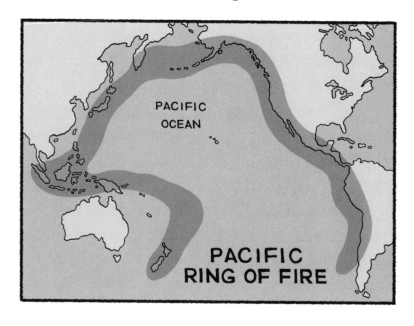

KIND OF CRUSTY!

The earth's crust isn't one solid piece like that peach skin. It's made up of different pieces, called plates. These pieces are "floating" on top of the mantle. They're constantly moving, like super-slow icebergs. The normal movement isn't noticeable—just like you can't see your hair growing—but it's always shifting very, very slightly. The edges of the plates are where the action is. Earthquakes happen where the edges of the plates slide past each other or bump into each other. @

Over on the East Coast, where the 2011 earthquake happened, there are no plates rubbing against each other. So what caused the earthquake? Scientists think it was the result of ancient **FAULTS** deep in the earth's crust.

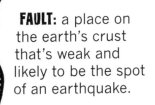

WORDS TO KNOW

FAULT: a place on the earth's crust that's weak and likely to be the spot of an earthquake.

IT'S NOT MY FAULT!

Imagine that you broke a dinner plate and glued it back together. The seam where you used the glue isn't going to be as strong as the solid plate around it. It's weaker there. That's what faults are like.

THE CRUST AT A FAULT HAS BEEN FRACTURED BY THE MOVEMENT OF THE EARTH. IT IS NOW WEAKER THAN UNBROKEN PARTS OF THE CRUST.

Pressure builds up at these fault lines because of the movement of the plates around them and in the mantle beneath.

WHEN THE PRESSURE GETS TOO GREAT, THE SEAM CAN SHIFT OR BUCKLE, CREATING AN EARTHQUAKE.

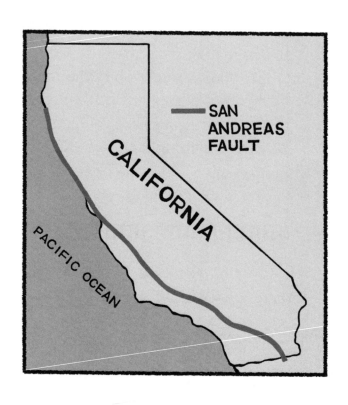

One big fault line in the United States is the San Andreas Fault. This group of faults runs almost the whole length of California. On the western side of the fault, the Pacific Plate is slowly creeping northward. On the eastern side, the North American Plate is sliding slowly southward. There have been several major earthquakes along this fault, like the 1906 earthquake that destroyed San Francisco and killed thousands of people.

DID YOU FEEL THAT?

Earthquakes can feel like a big truck rumbling down the street. Stronger earthquakes can knock things off shelves or even splash water out of your pool. Even larger earthquakes can topple buildings and destroy roads.

In the early 1930s, a scientist named Charles Richter developed a scale to measure the strength of an earthquake source. The Richter scale is based on how much the earth shakes during an earthquake. The ground motion is measured with a machine called a **SEISMOGRAPH**, and the strength of the earthquake is calculated using this information and the distance between the seismograph and the earthquake. Commonly called the Richter scale, each increase in the number on the scale means the strength of the earthquake goes up by 10.

WORDS TO KNOW

SEISMOGRAPH: an instrument that measures the movement of the earth's crust.

TNT: short for trinitrotoluene. A poisonous chemical mixture used as an explosive.

AN EARTHQUAKE WITH A MAGNITUDE OF 5 ON THE RICHTER SCALE MEANS THERE WAS 10 TIMES THE AMOUNT OF GROUND SHAKING AS IN A MAGNITUDE 4 EARTHQUAKE.

These might sound like small numbers, but it really adds up fast. If you blew up a handful of the explosive **TNT**, it would measure a 1.0 on the Richter scale. People wouldn't even notice the ground shaking (although they'd definitely hear the noise of the explosion!). But a magnitude 8.0 earthquake releases as much energy as exploding 6 million tons of TNT. That's how fast the Richter scale grows. Fortunately, most earthquakes are less than 2.5 and rarely felt at all.

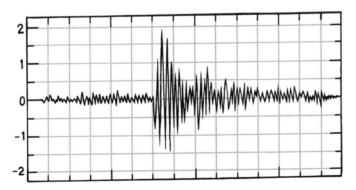
Recording of a seismograph on the Richter scale.

THE RICHTER SCALE

SCALE LEVEL	RESULT OF EARTHQUAKE
LESS THAN 2.0	People don't usually feel a quake this low on the scale. This would be about as strong as a small construction site blast.
2.0–3.9	The lower end of this range is usually not felt. People start feeling it at the higher end. There usually is no property damage.
4.0–4.9	Things will shake and rattle inside a building, but there won't be a lot of damage.
5.0–5.9	There is serious damage to buildings that are not well built. Buildings that are built well will have minor damage.
6.0–6.9	Large areas can experience serious damage to buildings.
7.0–7.9	This is considered a major earthquake, and can result in a lot of serious damage.
8.0–9.9	This is a huge earthquake. It can be devastating to a very large area, destroying buildings and roads.
10+	There has never been an earthquake recorded at this magnitude.

MOVE OVER, RICHTER (BUT NOT TOO FAR!)

Recently, scientists began using a slightly different scale to measure earthquakes than the Richter scale. Called the moment magnitude scale, it's a little different from the Richter scale. It does a better job measuring very large earthquakes because it has no upper limit. However, the moment magnitude scale has been less effective measuring smaller quakes. That's why the Richter scale is still used to measure earthquakes of less than 3.5, which is most of the earthquakes around the world. As new methods to estimate moment magnitude scale are developed, it will be used for those smaller earthquakes more and more. And for those rare big ones, the U.S. Geological Survey turns to the moment magnitude scale. ◎

A seismograph works by recording even the smallest vibrations in the earth. The equipment is hung, usually with springs. When the ground shakes, the machine itself remains relatively steady—because it's on the springs. But it records the movement of the ground beneath it.

DID YOU KNOW?

When they were first invented, the largest seismograph weighed about 15 tons.

WHERE DO WE BEGIN?

What happens when you throw a huge rock into the smooth, calm waters of a pool? There's an initial splash where the rock plunges into the water. Then waves spread out from around that point. Earthquake waves travel in the same way.

The place where the earthquake begins, where pressure moves the plates, for example, is called the **EPICENTER** of the earthquake. But it's not only the earth right above the earthquake that feels it. **SEISMIC WAVES** spread out from the epicenter, just like the waves of water in the pool.

WORDS TO KNOW

EPICENTER: the point on the earth's crust where an earthquake starts.

SEISMIC WAVES: the energy that travels outward from the epicenter of an earthquake.

SOME OF THESE WAVES CAN TRAVEL FOR MILES AND MILES.

If the epicenter of the earthquake happens to be under the ocean, there are no buildings or people to get hurt. But there is a whole different problem. If the earth deep underwater gets pushed up along a fault, all the water that's on top of that land gets pushed up too. It begins to move away from the epicenter. As it travels, the water loses speed closer to land, but it gets taller.

THIS ENORMOUS WAVE IS KNOWN AS A TSUNAMI.

A tsunami is a monster wave that can travel much farther inland than a typical wave. It is taller, stronger, and far more powerful, too. A tsunami can completely devastate an area.

In 2004, an earthquake in the Indian Ocean just off the coast of Sumatra triggered one of the most deadly natural disasters in recorded history. The earthquake was around a 9.1 on the Richter scale and lasted an unbelievable 8 to 10 minutes. It was the third-largest earthquake ever recorded and it launched a deadly tsunami.

WORDS TO KNOW

METEORITE: a piece of rock that falls from space and lands on Earth's surface.

POINT OF ORIGIN: the location where an earthquake begins.

RADIATION: energy that comes from a source and travels through something, like the radiation from an X-ray that travels through a person.

The tsunami traveled across the Indian Ocean, where it hit a dozen countries including Sri Lanka, India, and Thailand. Hundreds of thousands of people were killed, and huge areas were completely demolished.

DID YOU KNOW?

Scientists think a **METEORITE** may have created an enormous tsunami more than 3.5 billion years ago.

But earthquakes can trigger tsunamis much closer to their **POINT OF ORIGIN**, too. On March 11, 2011, a huge 9.0 earthquake struck off the coast of Japan, starting a horrible chain reaction of events. The massive undersea quake sent an enormous tsunami washing over the land, as high as 133 feet (over 40 meters) in some places. The wave caused major damage to Japan's nuclear power plants, creating a deadly danger from the threat of **RADIATION**. The entire situation was a devastating blow to the country—the worst earthquake ever to have hit Japan.

MAKE YOUR OWN
TSUNAMI SIMULATOR

SUPPLIES

* 2 large, deep rectangular aluminum pans, stacked inside each other for strength

* scissors

* old beach ball or rubber playground ball

* duct tape

* water

* someone to help hold your tsunami "ocean"

This project will help you see how an earthquake underneath all that ocean water can cause a major wave miles away. You may want to do this project outside. If there are any leaks or accidents, you don't want to flood your house!

1 Cut a window out of the bottom of each aluminum pan. Leave about a 1-inch rim around the edges (2½ centimeters).

2 Cut the beach or playground ball so you have one large, flat piece of plastic or rubber.

3 Turn the pan over. Using the duct tape, secure the piece of ball to the bottom of the pan, stretching it to cover the hole completely. You need to make sure you don't have any openings, or your ocean will leak! Place duct tape around the entire seam between the ball and the pan.

4 Turn the pan right-side-up so the cut ball is on the bottom of the pan.

15

5 Pour water into the pan. You don't want to fill it all the way up, or it will be too heavy and too wiggly to pick up. Pour in just enough water so your helper can hold the pan with two hands easily.

6 With your helper holding the tsunami pan above the ground, reach underneath with your fist. Position your fist at one end of the bottom of the pan, not in the middle or on the side. When you're both ready, gently punch the bottom of the pan.

7 You'll make a wave on one end of the pan that will roll to the other side of your "ocean." The harder you punch it—making a larger "earthquake"—the stronger your tsunami will be.

8 Experiment with different hits, taps, or punches, and see if there's a difference in the way the wave hits the "shore," or edges of the pan. This shows you how a tsunami can start in an earthquake, because of the water pushing up from underneath, and then travel to land very quickly.

MAKE YOUR OWN
SHAKE TABLE

SUPPLIES

❋ 2 large, stiff pieces of cardboard of equal size

❋ 4 balls of the same size (like golf balls)

❋ large rubber bands

❋ ground cover materials such as sand, dirt, or rocks *(optional)*

❋ building materials such as blocks, popsicle sticks, toothpicks, clay, or other materials

Architects and engineers who design buildings in areas prone to earthquakes try to create structures that will be stable if an earthquake hits. A shake table is used to shake a model and see what happens. It makes the same motion as an earthquake. You can see what it's like when you build your own shake table and then try to create structures that can withstand the force of moving earth beneath them.

1 Place the balls between the pieces of cardboard. Use the rubber bands to hold the pieces of cardboard together tightly. If your rubber bands can't stretch all the way around, make a chain by looping several rubber bands together.

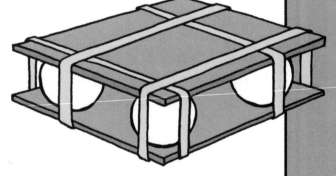

2 Put your shake table on a sturdy surface. If you're using ground cover, put that on the top board now.

3 Begin building. Use your building materials to create a structure a foot high or more (about 30 centimeters).

4 When you are done building, have a helper hold the bottom board steady while you gently pull or push on the top board. Let go and see what happens to your buildings. Experiment with different shapes and sizes of buildings.

5 What worked and what didn't? Try to make improvements until you can create a building that withstands your "earthquake." You might try creating "cross beams" with popsicle sticks on a square structure to make it sturdier. Or maybe you can provide supports inside a clay building. Are your buildings sturdier on one type of ground cover than another? Think about how structures in different areas of the world would be built, based on the likelihood of having an earthquake.

MAKE YOUR OWN
SEISMOGRAPH

SUPPLIES

❋ large cardboard box

❋ scissors

❋ long strip of paper (or cut thin strips of scrap paper and tape them together into a long strip)

❋ plastic or paper cup

❋ string

❋ felt-tip marker

❋ gravel, sand, or another weight (you may want clay, too, if you're using sand)

A seismograph helps scientists figure out exactly how strong a particular earthquake is. They use the data to try to predict future earthquakes and determine how to keep people safe during a strong earthquake. You can create a simple seismograph to understand how the real ones work.

1 Turn the box on its side so the opening is facing you. This will be the front of your seismograph.

2 About an inch from the bottom of the box (2½ centimeters), cut slits in the left and right walls in the center, wide enough for your strip of paper to pass through. Run the paper through one slit, across the box, and out the opening on the other side. Leave enough paper outside the box to act as your paper source during the "earthquake."

3 Poke 2 holes in the top center of the box. Then poke 2 holes on opposite sides of the cup, right below the rim. Poke one more hole in the bottom center of the cup big enough for the felt-tip marker to fit in snugly.

4 Run a piece of string through the holes in the box, then through the holes in the top of the cup, and tie them together. Don't put any string through the hole in the bottom of the cup. You want your cup to hang just an inch or two above the bottom of the box (2½ to 5 centimeters).

5 Stick your marker through the hole in the bottom of the cup. Position it so the tip just barely touches the paper beneath it.

6 Fill the cup with the sand or gravel to weight it down. (If you're using sand, you may want to plug around the marker with clay to keep the sand from leaking out.) Your cup should be hanging, unblocked, from the top of the box with the marker just touching the paper.

7 You're ready to shake! Have a friend or family member gently shake the box back and forth as you pull the paper strip through your seismograph. Pull it slowly and steadily. As the box shakes, the cup will swing, and the marker will measure the vibrations with marks on the paper. When you're finished, you'll have a graph of your "earthquake."

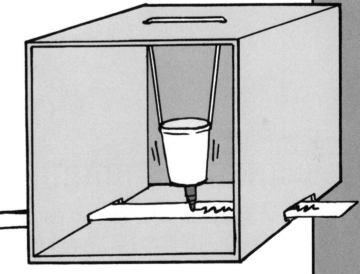

CHAPTER TWO
VOLCANOES

In 79 **CE**, the people of the Italian town of Pompeii were going about their daily business as usual. Everything changed when the nearby volcano, Mount Vesuvius, suddenly erupted. The ground rumbled and the skies darkened as ash and rocks rained down upon the town. Many people fled, but those who remained were buried in ash.

So much ash fell on Pompeii during the two-day eruption that the entire town was completely buried under 13 to 20 feet of ash and stone (4 to 6 meters). After rains fell, the ash hardened, and the entire city was completely forgotten for almost 1,700 years. When **ARCHAEOLOGISTS** stumbled upon it, they carefully **EXCAVATED** Pompeii. People were amazed to find that fateful day preserved in the ground. Hardened loaves of bread were still in ovens, and people and animals were frozen in the streets where they had fallen.

WORDS TO KNOW

CE: put after a date, CE stands for Common Era and counts up from zero. BCE stands for Before the Common Era and counts down to zero. These are non-religious terms that correspond to AD and BC.

ARCHAEOLOGIST: a scientist who studies ancient people through the objects they left behind.

EXCAVATE: to dig out material from the ground.

The eruption of Mount Vesuvius is one of the most dramatic volcanic eruptions in recorded time because of the way the town was buried and preserved. It created a frozen moment in time.

Do you picture volcanoes as hot, bubbly mountains that spew lava, ash, and smoke into the sky, night and day? When they are active, volcanoes can do all of these things.

BUT MOST VOLCANOES, MOST OF THE TIME, ARE MORE LIKE RESTING GIANTS THAT COULD WAKE UP AT ANY TIME.

DID YOU KNOW?

The word *volcano* comes from the Roman god of fire, Vulcan.

ARE YOU SLEEPING?

Like earthquakes, volcanoes are most common where the earth's plates meet each other. When one plate slides beneath another plate, the sinking plate is put under pressure and heats up. This releases hot gas and steam that heats and melts the rock above. This **MAGMA** rises to the surface and creates volcanoes.

WORDS TO KNOW

MAGMA: partially melted rock below the surface of the earth.

ACTIVE VOLCANO: a volcano that has erupted in recent recorded time.

Magma is super hot, usually around 1,300 to 2,400 degrees Fahrenheit (705 to 1,315 degrees Celsius). It's also lighter than solid rock, so it flows upward through the rock. And when it reaches the surface, *kapow!* It can come shooting through, erupting with amazing force. When the magma, called lava

when it's outside the volcano, slides over the surface of the earth, it very slowly cools. As the volcano continues to erupt and cool, the sides of the volcano can build up. When a volcano erupts often over time, it's considered to be an **ACTIVE VOLCANO**.

ACTIVE

DORMANT

EXTINCT

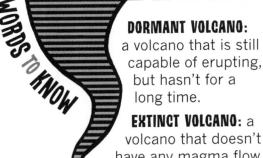

WORDS TO KNOW

DORMANT VOLCANO: a volcano that is still capable of erupting, but hasn't for a long time.

EXTINCT VOLCANO: a volcano that doesn't have any magma flow anymore, so it won't erupt again.

But sometimes, a volcano will become **DORMANT** and stop erupting for as long as hundreds of years. But just because a volcano is dormant doesn't mean it's never going to erupt again. It only means it hasn't erupted in a very long time, and isn't expected to erupt anytime soon. There is still magma bubbling inside it, and often steam is still coming out. Once a volcano hasn't erupted for thousands of years, it is labeled **EXTINCT**. There is only a very small chance of it ever erupting again.

DID YOU KNOW?

The tallest volcano in the solar system isn't even on Earth—it's on Mars, and it's over 14 miles tall (23 kilometers)!

WE'RE ALL DIFFERENT

Although volcanoes erupt in the same general way, the shape they form can look different. There are three basic shapes that volcanoes take: cone, shield, and stratovolcano.

WORDS TO KNOW

SLOPE: the slant of a mountain.

- **CONE:** This small volcano has straight sides with steep **SLOPES**. There's a large crater at the top where the lava flows out.

- **SHIELD:** This volcano has gentle slopes on the sides that almost curve outward.

- **STRATOVOLCANO:** This is a volcano you might draw in a dinosaur diagram, almost like a tall triangle. It has gentle lower slopes, but very steep upper slopes curving inward and upward at the top. It has a small crater at the very top where the lava flows out. ◉

CONE

SHIELD

STRATOVOLCANO

LARGEST RECENT ERUPTIONS

Although Pompeii was probably the most dramatic example of an eruption, there have been many other volcanoes in modern times that erupted and affected people living near them:

YEAR	VOLCANO	LOCATION
1783	Laki	Iceland
1815	Tambora	Indonesia
1883	Krakatau	Indonesia
1912	Katmai	Alaska
1991	Pinatubo	Philippines

The most powerful eruption in recorded history was Mt. Tambora in Indonesia. In 1815, it erupted with a power 52,000 times greater than the atomic bomb that destroyed Hiroshima, Japan, in World War II. The fine ash from the eruption stuck around in the atmosphere for three years, and affected the entire planet. In both North America and Europe, the ash kept temperatures so low that people called it the Year without a Summer.

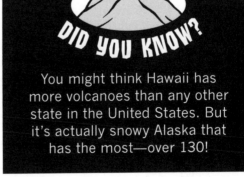

DID YOU KNOW?

You might think Hawaii has more volcanoes than any other state in the United States. But it's actually snowy Alaska that has the most—over 130!

WHAT'S COMING?

On May 18, 1980, Mount St. Helens in Washington State erupted, killing 57 people and nearly 7,000 big game animals like deer, elk, and bear. The eruption wasn't completely unexpected. The volcano had been dormant for over a hundred years, but in the months before the eruption, a series of earthquakes had made magma flow into the volcano. After the earthquakes started, the volcano began giving off small eruptions of steam and ash. Scientists started to think something was going to happen—but they didn't know exactly when, or how strong it would be.

WORDS TO KNOW

VOLCANOLOGIST: a scientist who studies volcanoes.

Scientists keep a close watch on most volcanoes that are located near human civilization. They try to predict whether or not there will be an eruption in the near future. They use seismographs to detect earthquakes that allow

magma to rise into volcanoes. They detect gasses that signal changes in the volcano. They measure the shape and size of the volcano to see if it's beginning to bulge (which Mount St. Helens had). All of these indicators give scientists an idea of whether a volcano is about to blow. But science is not perfect and **VOLCANOLOGISTS** keep improving their methods all the time.

LIFE AFTER AN ERUPTION

As you can guess, one of the big dangers from an erupting volcano is the burning hot lava. It can destroy buildings, swallow entire towns, and take lives. But lava is not the only danger from an eruption.

WORDS TO KNOW

FERTILE: land that is rich in **NUTRIENTS** and good for growing **CROPS**.

NUTRIENTS: substances that living things need to live and grow.

CROP: a plant grown for food and other uses.

MINERALS: nutrients found in rocks and soil that keep plants and animals healthy and growing.

The ash that spreads far from an eruption can make people sick, especially if it's thick and heavy. It can coat everything and make breathing a challenge. Eruptions also give off gases that can be dangerous to people and animals.

But after the danger has passed and the volcano has quieted down, the land around the volcano eventually becomes surprisingly **FERTILE**. The breakdown of the volcanic rocks and ash leaves behind soil rich in **MINERALS**.

SOME PEOPLE LIVE CLOSE TO A VOLCANO TO TAKE ADVANTAGE OF THE FERTILE SOIL— PUTTING THEMSELVES IN THE POSSIBLE DANGER ZONE.

MAKE YOUR OWN
VOLCANO MODELS

You can show your friends and family the different types of volcanoes with this project.

1 In a microwave-safe bowl, melt butter and marshmallows for two minutes. Stir, heat for another minute, and stir again.

2 In a very large bowl, mix together the rice cereal and marshmallow mixture until the cereal is completely coated.

3 You may want to put some butter on your hands to keep the cereal from sticking to your hands. Then, put a big pile of the mixture onto a large piece of waxed paper. Begin shaping the pile into one of the types of volcanoes—a cone, shield, or stratovolcano. Be sure to clearly make a crater.

4 Tint your frosting red for lava. Then "paint" it on your volcano, coming from the crater and running down the sides—just like flowing lava!

5 Enjoy your creation, and be sure to explain all about volcanoes to everyone who admires it!

MAKE YOUR OWN
ERUPTING VOLCANO

SUPPLIES

* ✳ cookie sheet
* ✳ cake baked in Bundt or tube pan
* ✳ vanilla frosting
* ✳ food coloring (brown, green, and red)
* ✳ drinking cup
* ✳ red gelatin
* ✳ funnel
* ✳ lemon juice
* ✳ 1 tablespoon baking soda (15 grams)

Why not make a cake that's a dessert and a science experiment all in one?

1 Put the baked cake on top of the cookie sheet, round side up. Scoop out some frosting and add brown food coloring. Do the same to make green and red frosting. Frost the cake brown for the volcano. Use green around the bottom edges for grass and red for lava around the opening.

2 Set your cup inside the hole of the cake, so that the very top of the cup just reaches the top of the opening. If you need to, put the cup on an inverted cup, or a stack of cookies, or anything that brings it to the right height.

3 Mix the red gelatin according to the package directions, and let it cool for about 15 minutes. You don't want it to firm up, but you don't want it steaming hot, either.

CUT-AWAY VIEW

4 Use the funnel to fill the cup halfway with the gelatin. Then add lemon juice until it's almost full.

5 When you're ready, drop the baking soda into the cup. Your family and friends will be amazed!

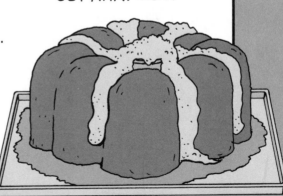

MAKE YOUR OWN
CAKE BATTER LAVA FLOW

The rate that lava flows down the sides of a volcano and threatens structures and life depends on the shape of the volcano. You can test the lava flow of different types of volcanoes with this project. Do not eat any of the cake batter! It will be dirty after you're finished making it flow over the landscape.

1 Mix water into the cake batter mix. Don't add oil, eggs, or any other ingredients from the directions on the box. Put in enough water to make it thick like a heavy cream, but not too runny or stiff. It's okay to have some lumps in it.

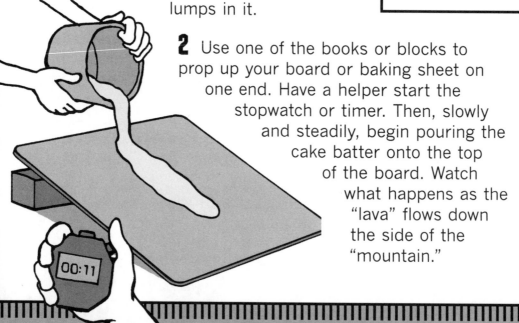

2 Use one of the books or blocks to prop up your board or baking sheet on one end. Have a helper start the stopwatch or timer. Then, slowly and steadily, begin pouring the cake batter onto the top of the board. Watch what happens as the "lava" flows down the side of the "mountain."

31

3 When most of the lava reaches the end of the board, stop the timer and write down the results. Take the ruler and measure the depth of the lava at different spots along the flow. And finally, take note of the shape of the flow. Is it a straight flow? Or does it spread out toward the bottom?

4 Use a spatula to scrape the cake batter back into the bowl. Repeat the experiment, this time propping the baking sheet or board up with both books or blocks Take the same measurements, and compare the results. Did the lava flow in a different pattern or depth? Was it faster? Did the speed of the flow make a difference in the measurements?

5 Volcanoes have different shapes. And that can make a big difference to the people and animals living near the volcano. It can be the difference between safety and danger if the volcano erupts.

CHAPTER THREE
TORNADOES

On Sunday, May 22, 2011, a massive storm began brewing and moving toward Joplin, a small town in southwestern Missouri. Late that afternoon, a **MULTIPLE-VORTEX TORNADO** unleashed on the town. It rapidly got stronger and moved eastward through the city. At its largest, it was over a mile wide (1.6 kilometers).

This devastating twister ripped bark from trees as it approached neighborhoods full of houses. The damage was **CATASTROPHIC**—almost every house was completely flattened or blown away.

When it was over, the storm left as many as 162 people dead, and the town was practically demolished. After looking at the damage, scientists declared the tornado the strongest category of tornado that can be measured today. It was the deadliest tornado to hit the United States since 1947.

TWISTER TIME

The next time you boil water, think of a tornado. Both require **CONVECTION**. Convection happens when warm air **MOLECULES** rise, then fall when they cool.

In a pot of water, the water at the bottom heats first and its molecules start to speed up and move around. The warm molecules then start pushing up through the cooler water molecules and soon water of different temperatures is swirling all around inside. Just pick up the lid and you'll see all sorts of motion!

The same thing is going on in the air. Air near the surface warms up from the heat rising off the ground. The warm air then rises and meets with cool air that is pushing down. This air movement, when combined with wind, can send a column of air spinning around.

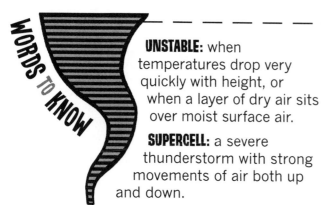

UNSTABLE: when temperatures drop very quickly with height, or when a layer of dry air sits over moist surface air.

SUPERCELL: a severe thunderstorm with strong movements of air both up and down.

Tornadoes are common during thunderstorms, when large air masses are **UNSTABLE**. In a **SUPERCELL** thunderstorm, when many tornadoes happen, the updraft of warm air can be as fast as 90 miles per hour (145 kilometers per hour)!

If a spinning column of air gets caught in this updraft, it will speed up even faster and create a cone shape. When a spinning, cone-shaped column of air reaches down from the clouds, it's called a funnel cloud. But when the rain and hail in a thunderstorm cause it to reach all the way to the ground, it's called a tornado. The faster the winds are blowing, the faster the tornado becomes.

WARM UPDRAFT

COOL AIR

COOL DOWNDRAFT

WARM AIR

TORNADO SAFETY

If you live in an area that's prone to tornadoes, make sure you know ahead of time what you'll do if there's a tornado warning. Have an emergency kit and know where it is. Get to a safe place—like a basement or interior room like a bathroom. Try to get under something solid that can protect you from flying debris. If you're outside, lie flat in a ditch or other low area. Don't stay in your car—it can get tossed around by strong tornadoes. 🌀

FUJITA SCALE

Tornadoes are measured using a scale that examines the damage done to man-made structures and the trees and plants in the area. **METEOROLOGISTS** and engineers look at the area after a possible tornado has gone through. They visit the site on the ground and examine it from the air, looking for things like swirl marks on the ground. They talk with eyewitnesses and look at radar reports. Once they've done their assessment, they give the tornado a rating.

WORDS TO KNOW

METEOROLOGIST: someone who studies weather and makes predictions about it.

For decades, experts measured tornadoes on the Fujita Scale. But in 2006, the National Weather Service unveiled a new scale, called the Enhanced Fujita Scale. It's very similar, but scientists hope it will provide a more accurate assessment of the damage and wind speed of tornadoes.

People have learned from past tornadoes and now build structures that they hope will better withstand the forces of a tornado. Many buildings will suffer less damage from the same winds. The new scale also added in more types of structures, as well as vegetation. Now scientists have a more accurate way to tell how strong tornadoes are.

NATURAL DISASTERS

ENHANCED FUJITA SCALE

LEVEL	WIND SPEED	WHAT HAPPENS
EF0	65–85 mph (105–137 kph)	Trees branches break, and there is some roof damage.
EF1	86–110 mph (138–177 kph)	Roofs start coming off, and moving cars can get pushed off roads.
EF2	111–135 mph (178–217 kph)	There is a lot of damage. Mobile homes are destroyed, train cars are pushed over, and large trees can be uprooted.
EF3	136–165 mph (218–266 kph)	Roofs and walls are torn off homes.
EF4	166–200 mph (267–322 kph)	Houses are destroyed and cars can be thrown.
EF5	>200 mph (>322 kph)	Strong homes can be lifted up, carried a great distance, and completely destroyed. Cars can be thrown through the air great distances, and concrete and steel structures can be badly damaged.

37

TORNADO OUTBREAK

If a storm system is large enough, it can cause more than one tornado on the same day. Or, if a storm system travels a great distance, different tornadoes can form and break up over a large area.

TORNADO OUTBREAK: a series of tornadoes that come from the same storm system.

WORDS TO KNOW

Generally, if there are six to ten tornadoes in the same weather system, it's called a **TORNADO OUTBREAK**. In order to be considered an outbreak, these tornadoes need to form in the same day, or start one day and last into the early morning hours of the next day. They have to be in the same region, too. If there's a gap of six hours before the next tornado, it's the start of a new event.

Normally, tornado outbreaks happen from March through June. Most outbreaks in the United States happen in Tornado Alley over the Great Plains, the Midwest, and the Southeast, where warm, moist air from the Gulf of Mexico pushes toward cool, dry air coming down from Canada.

DID YOU KNOW?

The largest tornado outbreak ever recorded may be the events that happened April 25–28, 2011, across the eastern half of the United States. There were as many as 327 tornadoes during those four days!

9:13 AM

1:07 PM

6:42 PM

HAVE A
BALLOON BATTLE

SUPPLIES

* 2 thin plastic bags (like a kitchen trash bag)
* thin wire or pipe cleaner
* glue or tape
* hot air popcorn popper or hair dryer
* 2 twist ties

Watch how hot and cold air masses interact with each other in this balloon battle. Think about how strong air masses must be to eventually create a spinning column of destructive air.

1 The thin plastic bag will be the body of your balloon. Use a wire or pipe cleaner to make the bottom of your balloon stay open by looping it in a circle and gluing or taping it to the opening of your balloon.

2 Have an adult hold the opening of your balloon over the hot air popper or hair dryer. You want to fill the balloon up with hot air. When you think it's ready, quickly close the bottom of the balloon with the twist tie (or squeeze the wire shut if you're using that) and release it. Your balloon will float up into the air!

3 Quickly fill and release a second balloon. Watch and see what happens as the air inside the balloons cool. Your first balloon should make its descent before the second one, as it cools down sooner.

4 The warmer air rising and cooler air falling that you see are the basic conditions that make tornadoes possible.

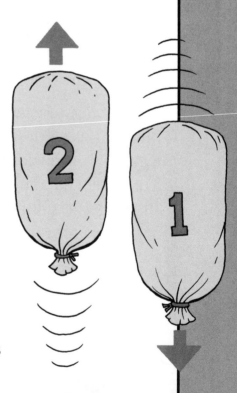

MAKE YOUR OWN
CONVECTION CURRENTS

In a thunderstorm, a body of warm air is forced to rise by an approaching mass of cold air. You can see how these convection currents form during thunderstorms with this experiment.

1 Fill the container with water and let it sit until it's completely still. If the water is still moving around when you start the experiment, it will affect your results.

2 When the water is completely calm, gently place a blue ice cube in the container at one end.

3 Then, add two drops of red food coloring to the water at the opposite end of the container.

4 Watch as one color rises and the other sinks. Why is that happening? You should see the water actually move from one place to another in the container. This is the convection that happens during a thunderstorm.

CONVECTION IN COLOR

SUPPLIES

* large, open-mouthed glass jar
* small plastic or paper cup
* hot and cold water
* food coloring
* plastic wrap
* rubber band
* tongs
* kitchen knife

Here's another chance to watch convection in action. You'll be able to see the movement of warm and cold molecules of water—similar to what happens with different temperatures of air masses. Have an adult help with the hot water and the knife.

1 Fill the large jar with cold water to within 2 inches of the top (5 centimeters). Set it aside.

2 Fill the small cup with very hot water. Add a few drops of food coloring.

3 Stretch a piece of plastic wrap over the top and secure it tightly with a rubber band.

4 Use the tongs to carefully lift the small cup and set it in the large jar of cold water.

5 Gently reach the knife into the water and cut a long slit in the plastic wrap.

6 The warm water inside the smaller cup will begin rising out through the cooler water. Then, as they cool, the warm water's molecules will move back closer together. You'll see the colored water begin drifting back down through the larger jar's water. This is the convection cycle—the rising and falling of warm and cool air.

CHAPTER FOUR
HURRICANES

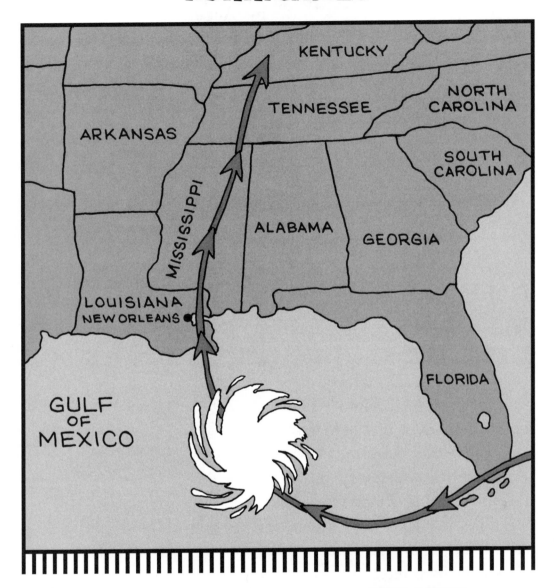

In late August 2005, people living along the **GULF COAST** of the United States began nervously keeping an eye on Hurricane Katrina. This strong storm had already crossed over southern Florida as a **CATEGORY** 1 hurricane. Some people lost their lives and there was flood damage. But as the hurricane moved over the warm waters of the Gulf of Mexico, it began picking up strength.

WORDS TO KNOW

GULF COAST: the states that are on the Gulf of Mexico, which include Texas, Louisiana, Mississippi, Alabama, and Florida.

CATEGORY: the word used to classify the strength of hurricanes, from one to five.

STORM SURGE: the sea water pushed along by a hurricane. It rushes inland and causes flooding when the storm reaches the coastline.

LEVEE: a wall, usually made of earth, that is built to hold back water.

By August 28, Katrina was a monster Category 5 hurricane. Meteorologists and residents along the Gulf Coast began preparing for a major hit—but it was still uncertain where the storm would make landfall.

On August 29, Hurricane Katrina slammed into the southeastern coast of Louisiana. Although the hurricane had weakened to a Category 3, it was still packing winds around 125 miles per hour (200 kilometers per hour). The **STORM SURGE** pushed ashore by the winds caused flooding as far inland as 12 miles (19 kilometers).

It was the worst possible outcome for the city of New Orleans and the residents along the coast. **LEVEES** that were supposed to protect residents were overwhelmed by the powerful rising floodwaters and began to collapse. Over 50 levees failed, and water surged into the city, submerging about 80 percent of New Orleans.

HURRICANES FORMING

A hurricane is a type of **TROPICAL CYCLONE** that occurs over the Atlantic Ocean, the Gulf of Mexico, and the eastern Pacific Ocean. A hurricane is also known as a **TYPHOON** or a **CYCLONE**, depending on where it occurs. But no matter the name or the place, they are all massive storms that can stretch up to 600 miles wide (966 kilometers) and pack spiraling winds that can reach close to 200 miles per hour (320 kilometers per hour).

How does a hurricane start? It begins over warm tropical ocean waters near the **EQUATOR**. When strong winds push warm, moist air upward, it leaves an area of low **AIR PRESSURE** near the surface. Air from the surrounding area swirls in to fill the space. Then that air is warmed and rises up. As the air rises, it starts to cool and forms clouds. The cycle continues, with more and more clouds growing and coming together.

WORDS TO KNOW

TROPICAL CYCLONE: any low-pressure system with swirling winds that starts over tropical or subtropical waters.

TYPHOON: the name of a hurricane over the western Pacific Ocean.

CYCLONE: the name of a hurricane over the Indian Ocean, the Bay of Bengal, and Australia.

EQUATOR: the imaginary line around the earth halfway between the North and South Poles.

AIR PRESSURE: the weight, or force, of the atmosphere in a place.

DID YOU KNOW?

Hurricane Katrina was a major natural disaster. Over 1,800 people died, and the property damage reached around $80 billion.

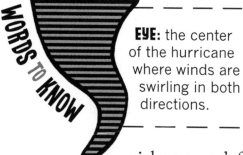

EYE: the center of the hurricane where winds are swirling in both directions.

The storm begins to spin and as it spins faster and faster, an **EYE** forms in the center. In the eye, there is very low air pressure, and it's calm and clear. In the meantime, as higher-pressure air from above flows down into it, the spinning picks up and forms a tropical storm.

ONCE THE WINDS FROM THE TROPICAL STORM REACH 74 MILES PER HOUR, IT IS OFFICIALLY A HURRICANE.

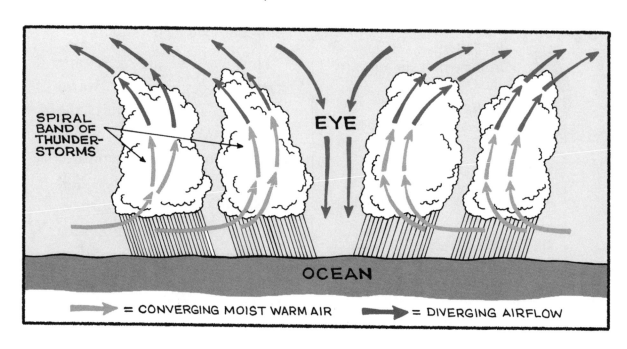

SPIRAL BAND OF THUNDER-STORMS

EYE

OCEAN

➡ = CONVERGING MOIST WARM AIR   ➡ = DIVERGING AIRFLOW

The whole storm—clouds, moisture, and wind—moves over the ocean until it either reaches cooler waters and breaks apart or touches down on land. It doesn't stay together long once it hits land, but it can do a lot of damage to coastal areas if it's a big storm.

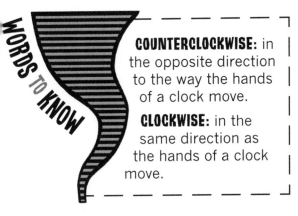

WORDS TO KNOW

COUNTERCLOCKWISE: in the opposite direction to the way the hands of a clock move.

CLOCKWISE: in the same direction as the hands of a clock move.

One reason the storm is so devastating is that the winds on the front, or leading side, of the storm are turning **COUNTERCLOCKWISE** around the eye. Then, as the storm moves along and the eye passes over an area, winds on the back end of the storm are spinning **CLOCKWISE**. Structures and vegetation that were just whipped in one direction are then whipped in the other direction. They're usually pretty weakened already from the first beating, so things can really get torn up with the second assault. And a hurricane can last for hours before it slowly moves on.

SURGING WATERS

Hurricanes can deliver a devastating one-two punch. In addition to the winds destroying structures and vegetation, they can also be powerful enough to push water inland from the ocean. Because the eye of the hurricane has wind swirling around it in all directions, it can pull water up and move it along with the storm. This water surges along with the storm, and when it reaches land, it comes rushing ashore.

THE SEAWATERS CAUSE MAJOR FLOODING AND CAN BE ONE OF THE MORE DEADLY ASPECTS OF A HURRICANE.

SAFFIR-SIMPSON HURRICANE SCALE

Like tornadoes, there's a scale to measure how big hurricanes are. It's called the Saffir-Simpson Hurricane Scale:

LEVEL	WIND SPEED	WHAT CAN HAPPEN
CATEGORY 1	74–95 mph (119–153 kph)	Mobile homes are toppled over, trees snap, there is flooding along coasts, and piers are damaged.
CATEGORY 2	96–110 mph (154–177 kph)	Houses can be lifted, mobile homes damaged, and trees can suffer a lot of damage.
CATEGORY 3	111–130 mph (178–209 kph)	This is a major hurricane. Damage to buildings is severe, mobile homes are destroyed, and there is a lot of flooding along the coast and a bit inland.
CATEGORY 4	131–155 mph (210–249 kph)	Many homes are completely destroyed, and flooding can happen far inland.
CATEGORY 5	>156 mph (>250 kph)	Buildings are completely destroyed and there is major flooding far inland. Much of the area sustains total destruction.

HURRICANE WARNINGS

TROPICAL STORM WATCH	A storm with winds around 39–74 mph is possible in your area within the next several days (63–119 kph).
TROPICAL STORM WARNING	Those tropical storm conditions are going to happen in your area within a day.
HURRICANE WATCH	A storm with winds of 74 mph or greater is possible in your area within the next several days (119 kph).
HURRICANE WARNING	Those hurricane conditions are going to happen in your area within 24 hours. You need to seek shelter immediately.

WORDS TO KNOW

SATELLITE: a device that orbits the earth to relay communication signals or transmit information.

RADAR: a device that detects objects by bouncing radio waves off them and measuring how long it takes for the waves to return.

GATHERING INFO

Scientists use **SATELLITES** and **RADAR** to track and gather information on hurricanes. But "hurricane hunters" with the National Oceanic and Atmospheric Administration (NOAA) fly through a storm to gather data. They check wind speeds, wind direction, and temperature to determine if the hurricane is building strength or weakening. It helps them figure out which direction the storm is heading.

Another thing hurricane hunters measure when they fly into a storm is the air pressure. A system of low pressure is what gets the storm started. The lower the air pressure drops, the stronger the storm. Lower pressure in the center of the storm means faster winds swooping in from areas of higher pressure.

HURRICANE SAFETY

With a tornado, you often don't have a lot of warning. But you do with a hurricane. Although scientists can't be exactly sure where a hurricane will make landfall or the path it will take, they can really narrow it down. And because a hurricane lasts for days, you can at least know several days ahead if you need to be alert and ready just in case.

To stay safe in a hurricane, try to move inland if you can. If you're vacationing at the beach, it might be tempting to get a thrill and watch the storm, but it's not a great idea. Storm surge and wind can be deadly. So pack up and move inland.

Prepare an emergency kit for your family. If the power goes out, you'll need to take care of yourselves. Depending on the strength of the storm, this can be for hours, days, or even a week or more!

MAKE YOUR OWN
MODEL HURRICANE

SUPPLIES
* paper clip
* string
* large, round bowl of water
* spoon

With this project, you can see how wind movement varies depending on where it is within the hurricane.

1 Tie the paper clip to the string.

2 Stir the water around in the bowl in one direction until you have a steady whirlpool going. This simulates the hurricane's winds swirling around.

3 Holding the end of the string, drop the paper clip into the water near the edge of the bowl. Does it get caught up in the moving water? This is what happens to anything that is in the winds in the outer band of a hurricane.

4 Pull out the paper clip. Stir the water again and lower the paper clip as close as you can to the center of the bowl. What happens? Is the paper clip moving faster or slower then when it was in the outside of the swirling motion?

MAKE YOUR OWN
BAROMETER

SUPPLIES
* balloon
* scissors
* glass jar
* rubber band
* straw
* tape
* paper
* marker

Air pressure is also known as barometric pressure. When barometric pressure starts to drop, look for winds and stormy weather. Barometric pressure is measured with a barometer. You can make your own barometer to see how air can have pressure that rises and falls as it presses down and lightens up.

1 Give the balloon some stretch by inflating it and then deflating it a couple times.

2 Cut the neck off the balloon and stretch the balloon over the mouth of the jar. Make sure the opening is covered with the balloon. Use the rubber band to hold the balloon in place.

3 Tape one end of the straw onto the balloon. Leave several inches of the straw sticking out to one side (7½ centimeters). This will be your measuring "needle."

4 Place the jar outside in a protected area. You don't want it to get rained on or blown over by the wind, so a covered porch or deck is great.

51

5 Tape the paper on the wall beside the jar. Use the marker to make a line where the straw is currently pointing.

6 Every day, see where the straw is pointing. When it moves up or down, make a line on the paper where the straw points. When the end of the straw points up, label it "high pressure." When it points down, label it "low pressure." What is making the straw rise and fall?

7 Try to impress your family by predicting the weather each morning using your barometer!

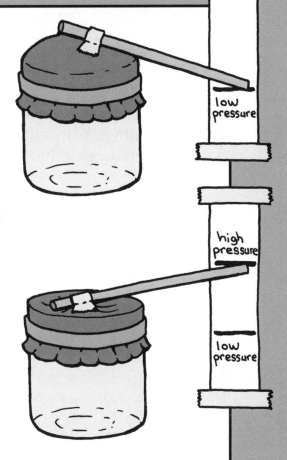

DID YOU KNOW?

Because there can be so many hurricanes in one season, they're given names so people don't get confused. There are six different lists of names. The list rotates each season and the names start over at "A" and go in alphabetical order. The names alternate between boy and girl names. If a storm turns out to be especially devastating or deadly, that name is retired and another name replaces it on the list.

MAKE YOUR OWN
WIND TUNNEL

Test different structures and strengths of buildings with this simple wind tunnel that simulates a hurricane's winds.

1 Cut out the short ends of the box, so it's solid on four sides and open on the short ends, like a tunnel.

2 Using the building materials, make different structures that are small enough to fit inside your wind tunnel. Secure them with clay, or think of other ways to hold them down. You could try taping them, or propping them up with toothpicks or popsicle sticks.

3 When you're ready, aim your fan on low speed into your wind tunnel. If your fan doesn't have speeds, start with it farther away, then move it closer to make the wind stronger.

4 What happens to the models inside the box? Try different types of structures and supports with different intensities of wind. You'll see how hard it can be for real-life engineers to construct buildings that stand up to hurricane-force winds!

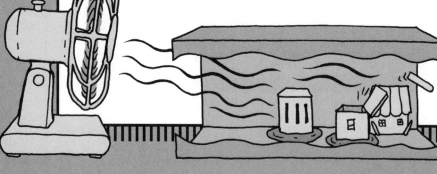

CHAPTER FIVE
FLOODS

In late August 2011, Hurricane Irene moved up the East Coast of the United States. The hurricane hit the Outer Banks of North Carolina before heading into Virginia. After that, it moved back out over the water and weakened into a tropical storm before heading for New England.

WORDS TO KNOW

SATURATED: full of moisture.

ABSORB: to soak up.

The storm made landfall around Coney Island in New York and left some wind and water damage, but Irene's real punch came when she moved up into the states of New York and Vermont. In one weekend, Irene dumped 7 inches of rain or more on Vermont in some places (38 centimeters). The soil was already heavily **SATURATED** from spring rains that had caused flooding, so this water had no place to go. Massive flooding washed out more than 200 roads and at least three historic bridges.

IT WAS THE WORST FLOODING TO HIT THE AREA IN ALMOST 100 YEARS, AND ONE OF THE TOP WEATHER-RELATED DISASTERS IN THE AREA'S HISTORY.

WHAT'S IT ABOUT?

A flood happens when water completely covers land that's normally dry. Sometimes it's moving water, like when a river rises up far past its banks. That water can still be flowing in the direction the river usually takes. Or, it can be water that swells up from a lake and just sits on land until it has someplace else to go. Heavy rains—or rains that fall so fast there's no time for the ground to **ABSORB** it all—can create pools of water on land. And sometimes these pools can be quite deep.

WHERE'S IT ALL COMING FROM?

Hurricanes aren't the only events that can flood land. Other reasons for floods include:

RUNOFF: If a really heavy amount of rain falls, or if the temperature warms up very quickly and a lot of snow melts all at once, all that water has to go somewhere. It can run down mountains or hills and flood into valleys or flat areas. Then it can take a while for the ground to absorb it all.

WORDS TO KNOW

DAM: a barrier constructed across a waterway to control the flow or raise the level of water.

STRUCTURAL FAILURE: Like the levees that broke in New Orleans after Hurricane Katrina, sometimes **DAMS** or structures meant to hold water in one place can fail. An earthquake can collapse a dam, or sometimes an engineering problem will make the dam weaker than it should have been. In the case of a dam or levee breaking, a sudden rush of a lot of water can flood an area downstream very quickly.

STORM SURGE: As happens during hurricanes, water can be pushed ashore by other strong storms. It doesn't have to be an official hurricane that's doing the pushing. Any storm-force winds that last even a short time can push water inland and cause flooding.

HUMAN ERROR: Sometimes workers will make a mistake when they're working on or near water lines. If a pipe gets cracked or bursts open, that water can cause a small flood in the nearby area.

WHAT HAPPENS NEXT?

When a farming area is flooded, planting and harvesting can come to a halt and food crops can be washed away or killed. Unfortunately, it can take weeks or longer for the water to finally recede. When a residential area is flooded, people can be forced out of their homes. They may not have a clear idea of the damage until the water dries up. And even then, the long-term effects can be devastating. People lose things that are important to them and cannot be replaced. Homes and businesses can't always be rebuilt, and when they can, it costs a lot of money.

DID YOU KNOW?

Just 6 inches of fast-moving water can knock you down (15 centimeters). And only 2 feet of water can float a large vehicle (60 centimeters)!

Other problems can last a while, too. Power to homes and businesses can be out for a long time. Traffic patterns are disrupted when roads are washed out or bridges are unsafe. The safety of drinking water can be affected if mud or **MICROORGANISMS** get washed into the drinking supply. In really hard-hit areas, disease-causing microorganisms can grow in standing water and infect people and animals.

Plants can be affected, too. Trees or other plants that are not meant to grow in water can die if they are submerged. Their roots rot or they can't get the nutrients they need.

MICROORGANISM: a life form that is so small it takes a microscope to see it.

TORRENT: a violently fast stream of water.

FLASH FLOOD: a sudden rush of water onto an area of land that is normally dry.

IT STARTS IN A FLASH

If a low-lying area suddenly gets a lot of heavy rain, or a **TORRENT** of water coming from snow melting, it can cause a **FLASH FLOOD**. That's when the increase of water is just much too fast to get absorbed in the ground or to go anywhere. It's called a flash flood when it happens in a time period of less than six hours (otherwise it's a regular flood).

Flash floods are dangerous because they can catch people completely off guard. You can drive to the store on a road that's perfectly fine, then on the way home, a sudden, intense storm can drop so much water that the road is flooded. Luckily, in most places flash floods are rare. ◎

HISTORICAL FLOODS

Hurricane Irene wasn't the first disastrous flood to hit Vermont. In 1927, Vermont had one of the most devastating floods in its history. That October, a lot more rain than normal fell on the state. When even more rain fell in November, the flooding began. Bridges, miles of roads, railroads, and homes were washed away. Records show that 84 people died.

There have been many devastating floods throughout history with an enormous impact on human life:

DEATH TOLL	FLOOD	LOCATION
2,500,000–3,700,000	1931 Central China floods	China
900,000–2,000,000	1887 Yellow River	China
500,000–700,000	1938 Yellow River	China
231,000	1975 Banqiao Dam failure	China
145,000	1935 Yangtze River	China
100,000	1530 St. Felix's	Netherlands
100,000	1971 Hanoi and Red River Delta	North Vietnam
100,000	1911 Yangtze River	China

Why have so many of these deadly floods been in China? The Yellow River was the culprit many times. But the worst of these floods was the 1931 flooding in central China, which is considered the deadliest natural disaster in history. The number of human lives lost was staggering.

Several factors contributed to the flooding. For many years before 1931, the area was in a long **DROUGHT**. Very little rain fell, and the vegetation was shriveled and dying, or dead. Then, heavy storms in the winter of 1930 left behind a lot of snow. When the snow melted the following spring, all that water made the rivers rise very high. Rain came in the summer of 1931, and there was a lot of it. There was so much water that all three of China's major rivers doubled in **VOLUME**. To make things worse, seven hurricanes hit the area in July. The normal rate is only two hurricanes in an entire year!

WORDS TO KNOW

DROUGHT: a long period of unusually low rainfall that can harm plants and animals.

VOLUME: the amount of space taken up by water or anything else that is three dimensional.

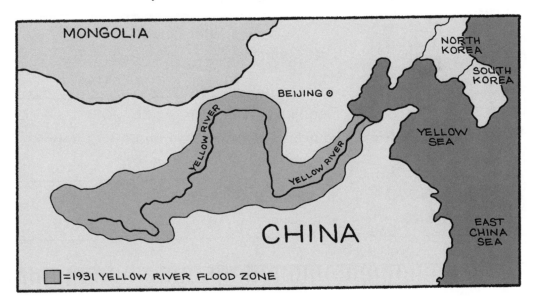

MONGOLIA

NORTH KOREA

SOUTH KOREA

BEIJING ⊙

YELLOW RIVER

YELLOW SEA

YELLOW RIVER

CHINA

EAST CHINA SEA

☐ = 1931 YELLOW RIVER FLOOD ZONE

All that water, combined with lack of vegetation to absorb it and hold it back, meant the rivers and runoff flooded the area. Structures that were supposed to hold back the water began to fail.

The Yellow River area of China is called the cradle of Chinese civilization. It's where a large portion of the population lives. All of those people were right in the path of the flooding. Then, after the flooding began, waterborne diseases began to take lives, too.

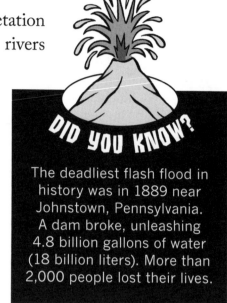

DID YOU KNOW?

The deadliest flash flood in history was in 1889 near Johnstown, Pennsylvania. A dam broke, unleashing 4.8 billion gallons of water (18 billion liters). More than 2,000 people lost their lives.

FLOOD WARNINGS

FLOOD WATCH	It's possible that a body of water in your area may overflow its banks.
FLASH FLOOD WATCH	Flash flooding is possible in your area. These watches can last as long as 12 hours.
FLOOD WARNING	Flooding is happening right now in your area, so stay alert and take safety precautions.
FLASH FLOOD WARNING	Flash flooding is happening right now in your area.

LONG-TERM EFFECTS

Although floods can damage homes and even take lives, there are actually some benefits, or good things, that come from small floods.

There are even areas of the world that are flooded as part of the natural weather cycle, and people have learned to live with it.

Floodwaters can bring needed water to deserts and other areas that are very dry during most of the year. Floods can also carry nutrients to lakes and rivers that help plants, fish, and other wildlife.

WORDS TO KNOW

NILE DELTA: a fan-shaped area of land in northeastern Egypt at the mouth of the Nile River where it empties into the Mediterranean Sea.

IRRIGATE: to supply land with water, usually for crops.

IN ANCIENT TIMES, THE PEOPLE WHO LIVED IN THE **NILE DELTA** LOOKED FORWARD TO THE YEARLY FLOODS. FLOODING HELPED **IRRIGATE** THEIR FIELDS AND BROUGHT FERTILE SOIL TO THE AREA SO THEY COULD GROW CROPS.

FLOOD SAFETY

As with other natural disasters, a safety kit packed and ready to go can help you a lot. If flooding happens, move to a safe place, which is usually higher ground. If you're stuck in your house, move to the highest floor. Don't walk across flooded roads or play in the floodwater. You can be swept away very easily, and you can't see what's under the water. You could step or trip on something dangerous. It is often hard to tell how deep the water is until it's too late.

It's critical to remember that in flash floods you should never, ever drive over a flooded road. The United States National Weather Service has a motto, "Turn around; don't drown." That's because so many people think, "Oh, it's just a little bit of water," and they try to drive over the road anyway. But that's often a deadly mistake. That little bit of water can lift your car and sweep it into deeper or faster-moving water. It's far better to be safe and find another route.

After a flood is over, listen to the radio or other news sources to find out if it's safe to drink the water. Also, be sure your electrical sources aren't near or under water, too. ◉

MAKE YOUR OWN
FLOOD PLAIN

Flooding can leave behind rich soil to grow crops. With this project, you can simulate a flood and grow your "crops."

1 Tear off a long, skinny piece of foil. Fold it to form a little river that is deep enough to hold some water, but no taller than the sides of your cookie sheet. Lay your river on the cookie sheet any way you'd like—through the middle, curvy or diagonal. You can fill your river with blue aquarium rocks.

2 Fill the area around the foil with potting soil. Be careful not to get the soil into your river. Pat it down firmly. Sprinkle some grass seed in the soil and cover it gently with a little more soil.

3 Flood your land by pouring water into your river. Keep filling it until it overflows its banks and floods onto your land. When you think the flood has watered your seeds enough, stop pouring. Put the cookie sheet in the sun until the soil is dry. Then, flood your river again.

4 Ancient Egyptians planted their seeds after the floodwater receded. They had to figure out a way to trap some of the floodwater to irrigate their crops later when the soil dried up. Try changing this project to collect some of the floodwater you pour into your river.

MAKE YOUR OWN
WATER-POWERED WHEEL

SUPPLIES

* four foam plates
* duct tape
* pencil
* small plastic or paper cups
* string
* straw
* plastic bag
* pebbles or sand
* water source (a hose or jugs of water)

It's hard to believe that just a little bit of moving water can knock you over—or even carry away something as heavy as a car! But you can see the power of moving water yourself when you create this simple water wheel.

1 Put two plates back-to-back and use the tape to attach them together. Do the same for the second two plates, so you'll have two sets of "wheels."

2 Use the pencil to poke a hole through the center of both sets of plates.

3 Tear off a piece of tape as long as the circumference of the plates. Place the tape down with the sticky side up. Line up the cups along the tape on their sides, all facing the same direction. Stick them to the tape, leaving about 2 inches of tape at each end of the strip (5 centimeters).

4 Wrap the strip of cups around one of the plate wheels, and secure the ends together. It should look like a water wheel now!

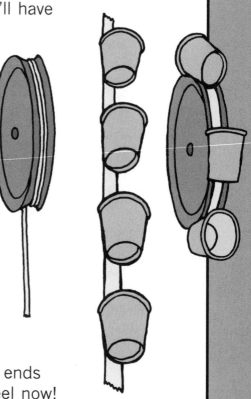

5 Secure the cups to the wheel by stretching a piece of tape over each cup and taping it to the sides of the plates. Then, using the tape, attach the second set of plates to your water wheel.

6 Cut a long piece of string. Tape one end of the string between the second set of plates and wind it around a few times, leaving most of the string trailing out. You'll be hanging your water wheel, so make the string long enough to pull something from that distance.

7 Slide the straw through the holes on both sets of plates. Then, thread a long piece of string through the straw, and use both ends of the string to hang your water wheel securely in an outdoor spot where it can spin, such as between the railings of a deck or porch stairs.

8 Place some pebbles or sand in the plastic bag and tape it securely to the end of the trailing string. This is what your water wheel will lift.

9 Use your water source to pour water into the cups to get the water wheel going. See how much weight your wheel can lift—you may be very surprised at the force!

MAKE YOUR OWN
ABSORBENCY PROJECT

SUPPLIES

✳ small clay plant pots with drain holes (all the same size) or paper cups

✳ saucers for each pot or cup

✳ different types of earthy material such as dirt, sand, peat, clay, potting soil, gravel

✳ measuring cup

✳ water

✳ pencil and paper

If the ground is completely saturated with water, rain or floodwaters will not be absorbed. But what type of earthy material is the most absorbent? You may want to do this project outside, since it could get a little messy.

1 If you're using paper cups, poke a dime-sized hole in the bottom of each one.

2 Fill each pot or cup with a different earthy material. Don't pack it in too tight, but be sure it's nice and firm. Set the containers onto their own saucers.

3 When you're ready, pour the same amount of water into each container. The amount of water you'll need depends on the size of your container. You want to use enough water so that it soaks well into the materials, but not so much that the soil is spilling out. Leave the containers overnight.

4 One at a time, carefully lift each container and pour any water in the saucer into the measuring cup. Write down how much drained out of each pot. The earthy material that has the least amount of "runoff" is the most absorbent.

67

CHAPTER SIX
DROUGHT AND HEAT WAVES

Imagine going outside and seeing nothing but dried-up soil, with few plants or trees for miles and miles. When the wind picks up, you have to run inside or cover your mouth and nose, because dust, sand, and dry dirt is whipped up and thick in the air.

That's the way it was in parts of the United States during the 1930s. The Great Plains—called the Dust Bowl during this time—was in a drought that lasted for years. Temperatures were unusually high. And farmers in the area didn't know yet that they should rotate their crops to keep the soil healthy and keep away pests and disease. They continued to grow the same crops year after year and cut down more and more trees to make space. This left the soil unhealthy, loose, and dry.

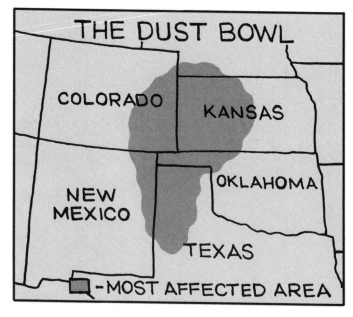

THE DUST BOWL

COLORADO

KANSAS

NEW MEXICO

OKLAHOMA

TEXAS

☐ -MOST AFFECTED AREA

ENTIRE SECTIONS OF COLORADO, NEW MEXICO, OKLAHOMA, KANSAS, AND TEXAS WERE JUST DRY, EMPTY AREAS OF OPEN WASTELAND THAT COULDN'T BE FARMED.

When the wind picked up, look out. The dust could choke you. In fact, April 14, 1935 became known as Black Sunday. On that day, the wind whipped up a dust storm so large it actually killed people in its path.

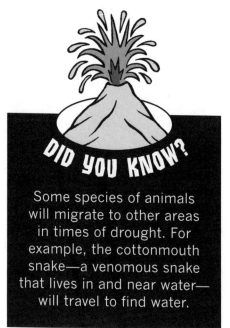

DID YOU KNOW?

Some species of animals will migrate to other areas in times of drought. For example, the cottonmouth snake—a venomous snake that lives in and near water—will travel to find water.

WHAT CAUSES DROUGHT?

Every part of the world has its own climate and weather patterns. Some areas, like the Sahara Desert, are used to long periods with little or no rain. Other areas, like the rain forests, are used to a lush landscape with regular bouts of heavy **PRECIPITATION**. And most areas fall somewhere in between. There's a fairly predictable pattern of rainy and dry times, usually tied in to the seasons.

WORDS TO KNOW

PRECIPITATION: the water that falls to the ground in the form of rain, snow, hail, mist, or sleet.

EL NIÑO: warming of the ocean surface off the western coast of South America that occurs every 4 to 12 years. It creates unusual weather patterns in different parts of the world.

BUT THE WEATHER ISN'T ALWAYS PREDICTABLE AND WHEN IT ISN'T, IT CAN CAUSE SERIOUS PROBLEMS.

Because of an overall warming climate, or weather patterns such as **EL NIÑO**, an area can receive below-normal amounts of rain. If an area is under an unusually long period of high air pressure, there will be a lack of precipitation. If there's too little water for a significant period of time, it might be a drought.

IS IT REALLY A DROUGHT?

Just because it hasn't rained in a few days doesn't mean you're in a drought.

METEOROLOGICAL DROUGHT: When an area hasn't received its normal amount of precipitation for an extended period of time. Life isn't impacted too much, but the area is at risk for a more serious drought.

AGRICULTURAL DROUGHT: If the crops in an area are struggling or failing because they aren't getting the amount of precipitation they need—or that they usually get—it's considered a drought.

DID YOU KNOW?

Special planes can carry "cloud seeding" equipment into clouds. They release substances that can jumpstart condensation in the clouds, hopefully causing rain. For the 2008 summer Olympics in Beijing, China, rockets were used to seed clouds before the opening ceremonies in hopes of keeping everyone dry during the rainy season event.

HYDROLOGICAL DROUGHT: When the water that's usually stored underground (sometimes deep underground) is running low, it's considered a drought.

SOCIOECONOMIC DROUGHT: When people begin being affected by water shortage, it's a drought. The impact on people can range from a ban on watering lawns or washing cars to having limited amounts of drinking water available.

NO WATER? BIG PROBLEMS.

Extended droughts can cause big problems for everyday life. After all, water is critical to our lives. Without it, everything can change.

- **CROPS FAIL**, which means less food for us and less food for **LIVESTOCK**, too. If it's bad enough, it can cause **FAMINE**, with entire populations starving.

- **WINDS BLOW AWAY DRY SOIL**, kicking up large dust storms and causing **EROSION**.

- **PLANTS AND ANIMALS SUFFER,** and entire **HABITATS** can dry up and be destroyed.

- **ENERGY SHORTAGES** can result if an area relies on water power from **HYDROELECTRIC** dams.

- **WILDFIRES BREAK OUT** because of the dry conditions, and can destroy homes and land.

WORDS TO KNOW

LIVESTOCK: animals kept by people to do work or for food.

FAMINE: a severe shortage of food.

EROSION: when land is worn away by wind or water.

HABITAT: the natural area where a plant or animal lives.

HYDROELECTRIC: generating electricity by water power.

WHERE'S THE RAIN, MAN?

It's natural for the environment to go through cycles of drought and heat waves, just like it's natural to go through times of flooding.

That's just the way life is on our planet. But scientists and engineers are always working to figure out ways to reduce the impact of these uncomfortable situations.

Dams are built to fill up **RESERVOIRS** of water. People can use that water for drinking or for crops in times of drought.

OCEAN WATER COVERS THE MAJORITY OF OUR PLANET. SCIENTISTS CAN **DESALINATE** THE OCEAN WATER, THEN USE IT TO IRRIGATE CROPS OR FOR DRINKING WATER.

Farmers now know how to rotate their crops in the fields they use. Different plants use different nutrients in the soil. When a different crop is planted each season, the soil can replenish itself. This helps minimize the kind of erosion that happened in the 1930s Dust Bowl. And farmers who live in areas that are likely to have droughts know to plant crops that aren't as dependent on water.

People can also collect rainwater using rain barrels. This water can be used to water gardens or even wash the dog!

WHAT CAUSES A HEAT WAVE?

Many times, droughts are tied together with heat waves. Of course, what's hot in one area is totally normal in another. If you lived in the desert of California, you'd be used to having hot, dry weather for long periods of time. But if you were visiting from Maine, where you're used to much cooler and wetter conditions, you'd think you'd traveled to some hot, distant planet!

So when does hot become a "heat wave"? The World Meteorological Organization (WMO) considers an area to be in a heat wave when the daily maximum temperature is higher than the normal maximum temperature by at least nine degrees Fahrenheit for more than five days in a row. A heat wave can last for weeks. And the air is often **HUMID** during a heat wave, which makes it feel even hotter and more uncomfortable.

The **HEAT INDEX** is the combination of air temperature plus the amount of humidity in the air. A very high heat index can be dangerous. When you're hot, you sweat to get rid of excess heat. The sweat on your skin **EVAPORATES** into the air and cools you down. But when it's really humid, moisture on your skin has a harder time evaporating since the air is already full of moisture.

WORDS TO KNOW

HUMID: a high level of moisture in the air.

HEAT INDEX: how hot it feels when you combine air temperature with humidity.

EVAPORATE: when a liquid heats up and changes into a gas, or vapor.

MON	TUE	WED	THU	FRI
☀	☀	☀	☀	☀
96	98	99	100	99
HOT	HOT	HOT	RECORD HIGH!	HOT

HEAT WAVE!

If your body can't cool down, and the heat index is high for a long period of time, you can get **HEAT STROKE**. You'll feel your heart pounding fast, and you'll start to feel dizzy. If you ever feel these symptoms it's very serious, and you need to get help quickly.

WORDS TO KNOW

HEAT STROKE: a dangerous condition that's caused when someone overheats because of high temperatures.

HEAT INDEX WARNINGS

90–105 DEGREES FAHRENHEIT (32–40.5 DEGREES CELSIUS)	Heat stroke is possible if you're outside too long.
105–130 DEGREES FAHRENHEIT (40.5–54.4 DEGREES CELSIUS)	Heat stroke is likely if you're outside too long.
130 DEGREES FAHRENHEIT (54.4 DEGREES CELSIUS) OR HIGHER	Heat stroke is highly likely if you're outside too long.
HEAT ADVISORY	Heat index 105–115 degrees Fahrenheit (46 degrees Celsius) for less than three hours.
EXCESSIVE HEAT WATCH	Heat index 115 degrees Fahrenheit (46 degrees Celsius) or greater for a few days.
EXCESSIVE HEAT WARNING	Heat index greater than 115 degrees Fahrenheit (46 degrees Celsius) for over three hours a day at least two days in a row.

MAKE YOUR OWN
RAIN BARREL

SUPPLIES

* water jug or a larger container if you have one (just be sure you can cut into the sides)
* small rocks
* funnel
* scissors
* duct tape

Whether you're planning for a drought or just want to conserve water, a rain barrel is a great way to take advantage of any rain in your area. This very simple, small rain "barrel" won't hold a lot of water, but it's a good start. Don't drink the water you capture and be sure others don't either!

1 Discard the cap from your water jug (or recycle it to use for another project).

2 Put the rocks into your jug. These will hold it down and keep it from blowing away when it's outside.

3 Insert the funnel into the neck of your jug. Secure the funnel with duct tape. The funnel will help maximize the amount of rainwater that your little barrel will catch.

4 Set your jug outside in an area that's protected enough that it won't blow away in strong winds, but where it will be sure to catch a lot of rain.

5 When the jug is getting full, use the water you captured to water your plants or garden. Replace the funnel and let Mother Nature fill your jug again.

MAKE YOUR OWN
DROUGHT LANDSCAPE

SUPPLIES

* ✱ fresh herbs from the grocery store or your garden
* ✱ paper towels
* ✱ flat tray
* ✱ sunny window
* ✱ glass spice jars

See just how devastating it is when plants are denied water during a drought. But in this case, you'll be able to still use them after your project!

1 Lay your fresh herbs out in a single layer on the paper towels, and set them all on a flat tray.

2 Position the tray by a sunny window. Check on the herbs every few hours. How fast do they dry out?

3 Try experimenting with the herbs. What if you put them in the shade instead of the sun? Do they dry faster if exposed to heat (like from the direct light of a desk lamp)? How much can they dry out and still be brought back to life a little bit with a spray of water? Some plants tolerate drought better than others.

4 When your herbs are totally dry, store them in small glass spice jars. Use them with the other spices in your kitchen when your family cooks.

CHAPTER SEVEN

WILDFIRES

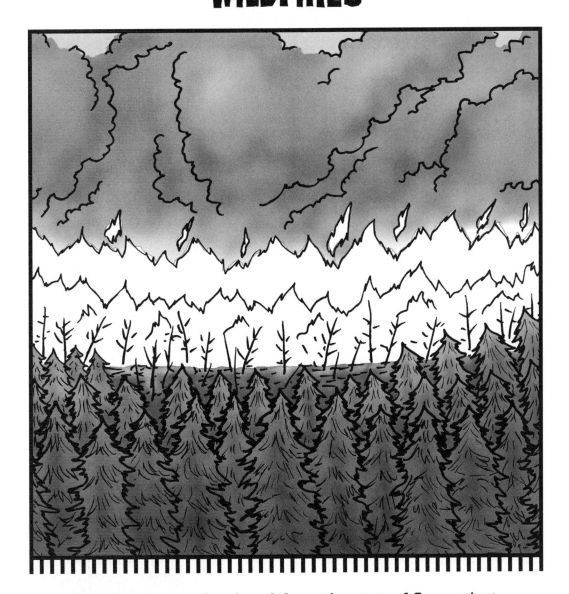

Imagine an area the size of the entire state of Connecticut
being burned to the ground. That's what happened during
the Great Fire of 1910, which is sometimes called the Big Burn.

In the summer of 1910, there was a drought in the northwestern part of the United States. The great forests in that area became extremely dry. Thousands of small fires began burning in different parts of the region, some sparked by hot cinders from locomotives and others by lightning.

Then, in late August, a cold **FRONT** came rushing in, pushing hurricane-force winds ahead of it. The winds whipped these small fires into larger ones. Eventually, the fires joined and became one massive **WILDFIRE**. This raging fire stretched from the state of Washington into Idaho and Montana. There weren't enough firefighters to battle the flames and the fire burned for over two days. Eventually the cold front brought steady, soaking rain that put it out. But before it was over, 87 people lost their lives, and about three million acres of land were burned (1¼ million hectares).

THE GREAT FIRE IS CONSIDERED THE LARGEST FIRE IN UNITED STATES HISTORY.

FIRES ARE BURNING

A wildfire is a large area of burning land that is often out of control or very difficult to contain. There can be many different reasons that a wildfire starts.

DID YOU KNOW?

Smoke from the Great Fire of 1910 reached all the way across the country to New England. **SOOT** traveled as far as Greenland!

ARSONIST: someone who deliberately sets a fire to property that doesn't belong to them.

Sometimes simple campfires can get out of control if the land around them is too dry or if campers don't put the fire out completely before leaving it. Kids playing with matches or lighters can start an entire wildfire. A carelessly flicked cigarette can start a fire. And sometimes, an **ARSONIST** starts a fire on purpose.

BUT THE BIGGEST CAUSE OF WILDFIRES ISN'T MAN—IT'S NATURE.

Almost a quarter of all wildfires are started by a lightning strike on dry vegetation. Many times, no one notices when a fire begins. But if it's dry and windy, the conditions are right for the fire to spread quickly. High temperatures and dry vegetation will easily feed a fire and help it grow. If it's autumn, dry leaves and fallen branches cover the ground. Dry grasslands are perfect for fires, too.

UNDER THESE CONDITIONS, HOMES
AND LARGE AREAS OF LAND CAN
BE IN DANGER OF BURNING.

SANTA ANA WINDS

If you're from Southern California, you've grown up with the Santa Ana winds. These are hot, dry winds from the northeast or east that come blowing in late fall and early winter. They can stoke fires and quickly make trouble. They're not just a little breeze, either. They can blow at 40 miles per hour (64 kilometers per hour).

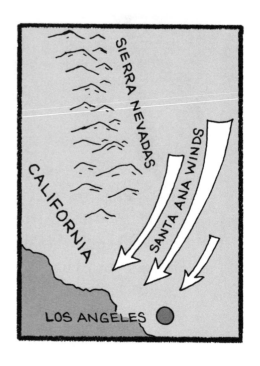

The Santa Anas start in the desert on the eastern side of the mountains. The wind begins as dry air over the Mojave Desert. When it travels up to the top of the mountains between the desert and the coast, the lack of air pressure in high **ALTITUDE** cools the winds down. But then, as the winds drop back down the other side of the mountains toward the coast, the air rapidly heats up because of the sudden increase in air pressure. There's more air pressing down on it than there was way up in the mountains. This dense, hot air comes blasting into Southern California, sometimes reaching hurricane force. Any small wildfire that happens to be in its path quickly becomes an **INFERNO**.

WORDS TO KNOW

ALTITUDE: the height of something above the level of the sea. Also called elevation.

INFERNO: a large fire that is dangerously out of control.

TYPES OF WILDFIRES

Not all wildfires are the same. They burn in different areas and some move faster or slower than others.

- **SURFACE FIRES** are the most common type of wildfire. They move along the forest floor slowly, fueled by dry vegetation, grass, and shrubbery.

- **GROUND FIRES** are usually started by lightning. They burn by **SMOLDERING** in a slow, steady burn. They consume roots that are often underground or other buried **FLAMMABLES**. They can burn for days or even months.

- **CROWN FIRES** are sometimes called aerial fires. They burn material high above ground, like the branches of tall trees or vines and mosses that are up in trees.

WORDS TO KNOW

SMOLDERING: when a fire is burning very slowly, possibly without any visible flames coming up.

FLAMMABLE: something that easily catches on fire.

SURFACE FIRE

GROUND FIRE

CROWN FIRE

FIREFIGHTERS

Putting out a big forest fire can be very difficult. Firefighters use different types of equipment and techniques to battle the blaze.

A PULASKI is a tool with an axe head on one side and a kind of flattened, sharp hoe on the other. Firefighters use it to dig soil and chop wood. They dig a fire line, or a strip of land that's clear of anything that can burn. Then, when the fire reaches this fire line, there's nothing there to fuel it and it burns itself out.

PLANES AND HELICOPTERS can carry a fire-retardant chemical or gallons of water to dump on fires from the air.

DID YOU KNOW?

Firefighters call the pink chemical they drop from planes to put out wildfires "sky jello" or "mud."

FIRE TORNADO

If flames are caught in air currents that are moving in opposite directions, a fire tornado can form. Fire tornadoes, also known as fire whirls, fire devils, or firenados, are similar to regular tornadoes, but made from fire. They're twisty whirlwinds that move quickly and spin, sometimes even moving away from the main fire itself. Most fire tornadoes are small, spreading about 1 to 3 feet wide (⅓ to 1 meter) and five to ten stories tall. Sometimes, though, they can get dozens of feet wide and more than 100 stories tall! The fastest ones spin at 300 miles per hour (483 kilometers per hour).

BATTLING BLAZES—GOOD OR BAD?

After the devastating fire of 1910, people thought the U.S. Forest Service should prevent and put out every wildfire. After all, millions of acres of land had burned. But others argue that wildfires are a necessary part of the environment.

WORDS TO KNOW

UNDERBRUSH: shrubs and small trees that grow beneath the taller trees in a forest.

Fires occur naturally in nature, such as from lightning strikes, and there are good reasons for that. After a while, the soil left behind after a burn is richer and has more nutrients than it did before. The fires burn out old, dead **UNDERBRUSH**, giving new plants a chance to grow. And clearing away the underbrush that can compete with larger, slower-growing vegetation, like trees, gives those bigger plants a better chance at survival as well.

WORDS TO KNOW

EVOLVE: to change or develop slowly, over time.

FIRE TOLERANT: able to survive being burned in a fire.

FIRE-RESISTANT: difficult to burn.

Some plants have actually **EVOLVED** to cope with fire. They may have flammable oils in their leaves that encourage a quick, hot fire. Then the fire activates their seeds to begin growing. That way, the young plants can start to grow without a lot of competition from other plants. This gives them a chance for survival that they might not have had without the fire.

Other plants are **FIRE TOLERANT**, like some that grow in Australia. These plants can withstand some burning without dying off. After being damaged by fire, they recover and continue to grow.

And there are some plants that are **FIRE-RESISTANT**. They don't suffer much damage at all during a fire. Because the big ponderosa pine is so tall, any flammable parts are high above surface fires and safe from burning.

DID YOU KNOW?

Over 100 peat fires—underground fires that are burning old organic materials—have been burning in parts of Indonesia since 1997!

FIRE SPOTTING

In hot, dry conditions, forest rangers stay alert for any possible sign of fire. The faster a fire is spotted, the safer everyone will be. Sometimes, the rangers decide the safest thing to do is let the fire burn itself out.

IF HELP IS NEEDED TO PUT THE FIRE OUT OR PROTECT CERTAIN AREAS, QUICK ACTION IS IMPORTANT.

Some forests have tall fire towers. These lookouts are staffed by people looking for any sign of fire in a heavily wooded area. There are also airplane patrols and public telephone hotlines so people can report anything they see.

WILDFIRE SAFETY

Have a family meeting long before any threat of wildfire to talk about a fire safety plan. You can consider planting some fire-resistant plants around your home to reduce the chances of your own plants helping to spread a fire. Be sure you have a disaster kit in your home and car. And stay alert during hot, dry weather for any warnings on the radio, television, or the Internet. ⊚

If you see a sign indicating a level of fire danger, it's not just a guess! To determine the risk level in an area, there's a scale that looks at the humidity of the air (dry air means more fire potential), the temperature (hotter temperatures could mean more likelihood of fires), recent precipitation (if it's rained during the last 24 hours, chances are lower for fires), and the speed of the wind (because the wind can blow flames and spread fires). You'll see fire danger rated as low, moderate, high, very high, or extreme.

IF YOU'RE CAMPING IN A HIGH-RISK AREA, BE EXTRA CAREFUL ABOUT PUTTING OUT YOUR CAMPFIRES COMPLETELY—OR DON'T START A FIRE AT ALL.

TODAY'S FIRE DANGER

LOW MODERATE HIGH VERY HIGH EXTREME

HIGH

1871 PESHTIGO FIRE

The deadliest fire in United States history was the 1871 Peshtigo Fire in Wisconsin. It burned 1,875 square miles of land (4,856 square kilometers) and took as many as 2,500 lives. On the same day, the better-known Great Chicago Fire burned 4 square miles (6½ square kilometers) and killed hundreds of people.

MAKE YOUR OWN
FIRE LINE

SUPPLIES
* tissue paper or newspaper
* large, shallow pan
* spray bottle
* water
* red food coloring

One of the ways that firefighters battle wildfires is by digging a fire line. Here's how you can do a test "fire line."

1 Shred the tissue paper or newspaper into small pieces and scatter them in the pan. Distribute evenly across the pan until the layer is about an inch thick (at least 2½ centimeters).

2 Run your finger through the shredded paper to dig out a trench. You want to create an area where there isn't any shredded paper.

3 Fill your spray bottle with water and add a few drops of food coloring—this will simulate your fire. Squirt one side of your fire line. This represents the fire burning. You don't need to squirt much—the water will spread through the tissue paper or newspaper by itself, kind of like a growing fire.

4 Watch what happens when it reaches your "fire line." Just like a fire, the water stops spreading. If it didn't work, ask yourself why, and see what you can do to change the outcome. Try spraying water more heavily on the center shredded paper and see what happens when your "fire" rages even more.

MAKE YOUR OWN
FIRE ESCAPE PLAN

If you live in an area with the potential for wildfires, you want to be sure to have a fire escape plan in place with your family. But even if your home wouldn't potentially be threatened by wildfire, having a home fire escape plan is a great idea. It can keep your family safe in case of a house fire, too.

1 On the paper, in an upper corner, write the number for your local fire department with the marker. Then, draw a diagram of the floor plan of your house. If you'd rather create this on the computer, you can do that instead. Be sure to draw in all doors and windows.

2 Mark the location of all the smoke alarms in the house. You should have one in each bedroom, one in the hall outside the bedrooms, and one on every level of the house. Don't forget the basement if you have one!

3 Then, call a family meeting. Explain the importance of having a fire safety plan for the family in case of an emergency.

DID YOU KNOW?

Wildfires happen on every continent except one. Can you guess which one? If you guessed Antarctica, you're right! There's not enough flammable material on that snowy continent.

4 Work together, using your diagram, to identify TWO ways out of each room. If you find that an upstairs window is one option, be sure to have a fire safety ladder in that room, or have a plan to get down from there.

5 Pick a safe family place outside to meet so everyone knows that you're all there. You might want to meet on a neighbor's porch (ask them first, of course!) or by a big tree that's away from the house.

6 Practice your safety plan at least twice a year.

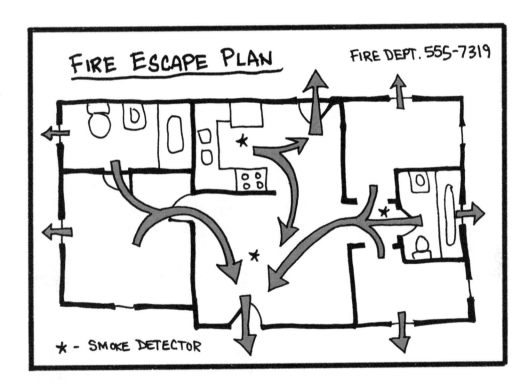

FIRE ESCAPE PLAN   FIRE DEPT. 555-7319

* - SMOKE DETECTOR

CHAPTER EIGHT
BLIZZARDS AND AVALANCHES

If you look out the window and see a ton of snow coming down, you might get excited that school will be cancelled for the day. Or you might start making plans for an epic snow fort or ski trip. But what if the snow kept coming? And coming? To the point where you couldn't leave your house for days, and your power went out? Most likely, that's not just a snowstorm. You're in the middle of a blizzard!

In 1888, one of the most severe blizzards in recorded U.S. history hit the East Coast. From New York to New Jersey, Massachusetts, and Connecticut, snow fell at record rates. Between March 11 and March 14, 40 to 50 inches of snow fell (102 to 127 centimeters). Winds howled at over 45 miles per hour (72 kilometers per hour). The **SNOWDRIFTS** were more than 50 feet deep (15 meters)!

WORDS TO KNOW

SNOWDRIFT: a bank of deep snow heaped up by the wind.

People were stuck in their homes for a week. Overhead wires snapped, causing power shortages and fire danger. The storm was called the Great White Hurricane, and the entire East Coast was practically shut down. Travel was virtually impossible, and the snowdrifts took more than a week to clear away.

When all that snow finally melted, it created big flooding problems. The people of New York City even tried to push the snow into the Atlantic Ocean to get rid of it!

IN THE END, MORE THAN 400 PEOPLE DIED DURING THE BLIZZARD.

But the deadliest blizzard in the world happened in 1972. For almost a week, winter storms battered villages in Iran. The area was buried in as much as 26 feet of snow (8 meters). Entire villages were wiped out and at least 4,000 people lost their lives.

THE MAKING OF A BLIZZARD

Heavy snowfall is not the only weather condition needed to make a blizzard. Believe it or not, there have even been "ground blizzards" when no snow is falling at all. The National Weather Service considers a storm a blizzard if there are large amounts of blowing snow combined with winds over 35 miles per hour (56 kilometers per hour). To be considered a blizzard, the **VISIBILITY** has to be less than ¼ mile for at least three hours (less than ½ kilometer). All that blowing snow can make it almost impossible to see where you're going—a condition called a **WHITEOUT**.

WORDS TO KNOW

VISIBILITY: the distance we can see in the light and weather conditions.

WHITEOUT: the condition in blizzards where you can't see anything because of blowing snow.

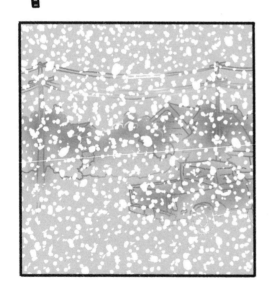

Most blizzards start as heavy snowstorms. For the snowstorm to become a blizzard, three things need to happen. First, the temperature has to be below freezing both at ground level and up in the clouds where the snowflakes form. If it's not below freezing at the ground, you'll just end up with rain or freezing rain. Freezing rain is no fun, but it's not a blizzard.

The next thing that's needed to make a blizzard is moisture. In winter storms, when wind blows over the water of lakes or oceans, some of the water evaporates and turns into water vapor. The water vapor makes the air moist and snow can form.

Finally, a blizzard requires warm, rising air. It seems strange that warm air would be any part of a blizzard, but it's the warm air that rises over cold air that's the key. When that warm air rises up, it forms clouds. And when the warm air meets the cold air, it forms a front. That's when that moisture turns into precipitation—in this case, snow.

BLIZZARD SAFETY

During a blizzard, if you stay inside, you should be safe. When people are injured in a blizzard, it's usually because of the cold or trying to travel in unsafe conditions.

WORDS TO KNOW

WIND CHILL: the temperature it feels like when you combine the air temperature with the wind speed.

FROSTBITE: damage that can happen to your exposed skin when you're out in freezing temperatures.

When you're outside in the cold and wind, the **WIND CHILL** makes it feel like it's colder than the actual air temperature. Cold temperatures combined with wind can be deadly very quickly. Any exposed skin can get **FROSTBITE**. The greatest risk of frostbite is when temperatures are less than 32 degrees Fahrenheit (0 Celsius).

So if there is a blizzard warning where you live, stay indoors and have some hot chocolate. If you have a fire in your fireplace or wood stove, be sure an adult checks the chimney for obstructions. Don't travel until the blizzard is over and roads are plowed. When you do venture out, be sure to dress in layers to stay warm. Cover up any exposed skin to prevent frostbite, too. ◎

BLIZZARD WARNINGS

WINTER WEATHER ADVISORY	There is the possibility of lots of snow, freezing rain, and sleet that can be dangerous.
WINTER STORM WATCH	Within 12–48 hours, there could be serious winter weather, like a blizzard or heavy freezing rain, sleet, or snow.
WINTER STORM WARNING	Weather conditions are hazardous due to heavy freezing rain, sleet, or snow.
BLIZZARD WARNING	Winds are over 35 miles per hour (56 kph here) and falling or blowing snow drops the visibility to ¼ mile.
WIND CHILL ADVISORY	Wind chill between –15 and –24 degrees Fahrenheit (–26 to –31 degrees Celsius).
WIND CHILL WARNING	Wind chill under –25 degrees Fahrenheit (–32 degrees Celsius).

LISTEN TO THE WEATHER SERVICE WARNINGS TO STAY SAFE IN BAD WINTER WEATHER.

DID YOU KNOW?

You can get stuck in a whiteout even if it isn't snowing. Major storms can make a dry, light, powdery snow. When the wind picks up, that snow blows around and creates the whiteout.

AVALANCHES

Another dangerous natural disaster that is caused by snow is an avalanche. An avalanche happens when a large, moving mass of snow tumbles down a hill or mountain. A lot of debris can be carried by the snow, like ice, rocks, and even uprooted trees.

Every year in the United States, about 100,000 avalanches come barreling down mountainsides. People skiing, snowboarding, or snowmobiling are some of the 300 people who are caught in avalanches every year. Fortunately, most of them survive, although an unlucky few do not.

VIBRATIONS OR GRAVITY CAN TRIGGER AVALANCHES.

AVALANCHE AIRBAG

Have you ever opened a box of cereal that has big, dried strawberries in it, and found all the berries are at the top of the box? That's

because objects that are larger will rise through particles or pieces around it that are smaller. That's how avalanche airbags are supposed to work. If someone is tumbling through an avalanche of snow, larger objects (like tree branches or rocks) will generally work their way toward the top of the moving pile. If a person activates an airbag, it will help make them larger, moving them closer to the surface. ◉

WELLINGTON AVALANCHE

On March 1, 1910, the worst avalanche in United States history hit the small town of Wellington, Washington. For days, a blizzard had piled as much as a foot of snow every hour on the area (30 centimeters per hour). Two trains were stuck on the tracks, unable to travel any farther.

Finally, the snow stopped. A rain began, along with a warm wind. On March 1, a lightning strike broke a slab of snow free during a thunderstorm. A massive section of snow—10 feet high (3 meters), a half-mile long (1 kilometer), and a quarter-mile wide (½ kilometer)—barreled toward town. The avalanche hit the trains, throwing them downhill, killing 96.

DID YOU KNOW?

Avalanches can reach speeds of 245 miles per hour (394 kilometers per hour). That's faster than a NASCAR race car!

The recipe for an avalanche is the height of a mountain combined with the steepness of its slope and the type of snow on it. A snow pile or snowdrift can begin forming on the side or top of a mountain. After a while, because of melting or because the snow becomes too top-heavy, it's in danger of letting go and rumbling down the side of the mountain. Avalanches can also start when additional weight is added to a weak layer of snow too quickly. This can happen during a heavy snowfall, from wind depositing too much snow too quickly, or even from the weight of a person.

AVALANCHE SAFETY

There are precautions you can take to avoid an avalanche and to increase your chances of survival if you're caught in one. Recreational areas post warnings about places to stay out of if they suspect the snow cover is unstable. Pay attention to those warnings and do not enter an avalanche danger zone.

If you're traveling in avalanche-prone areas, you need to have the right safety gear, such as an avalanche airbag. Without an airbag, you should grab on to branches or trees if you can. If the tree stays put, you can hang on to it until the avalanche passes.

WORDS TO KNOW

BEACON: a device that sends out a signal, indicating location.

Once the avalanche stops moving, the snow settles and packs down quickly. That's when another device is vital—a **BEACON**. This transmitter sends out a radio signal so rescuers can receive it and help locate the buried person quickly. ◉

MAKE YOUR OWN
INSULATION PROJECT

SUPPLIES

✳ tray or big dish

✳ ice cubes

✳ insulation materials
   to test (try things
   like newspaper,
   foil, plastic wrap,
   napkins, and fabric)

✳ rubber bands

One of the big dangers to people during blizzards is becoming too cold. As long as you stay inside, you should be okay. But if the power goes out, some homes lose their heat source. It's important to bundle up in that case by wrapping up with layers of blankets and clothing. This project will help you learn what materials are best for staying warm.

1 Before you start, be sure your ice cubes are all the same size. You're going to see which melts faster, so it's not fair if one starts out bigger!

2 Take a piece of your testing material and wrap it firmly around one ice cube. Fasten it with rubber bands to keep it completely wrapped. Return each wrapped ice cube to the freezer while you complete step 3.

3 Repeat step 2 with the rest of your ice cubes and materials.

4 Set all the wrapped ice cubes on the dish or tray, spacing them apart so they're not touching each other. Then leave them alone.

5 Come back to check on them every 15 minutes. You might be able to tell which ones are melting faster because of the size of the puddles around them. But sometimes the water gets absorbed into the materials wrapping them, so you'll have to see which cubes are really getting smaller.

6 After an hour or two (or three) whichever cubes are still largest are the ones that were wrapped in the most insulating material. Keep this in mind if you're ever cold. You want to wrap yourself in the material that will keep your body heat in!

DID YOU KNOW?

Cotton holds sweat and makes a very poor choice of clothing for doing anything active in cold weather. You may hear people say that in winter "cotton kills."

MAKE YOUR OWN
AVALANCHE EXPERIMENT

SUPPLIES

* clear jar with lid
* dry rice
* objects of different sizes (marbles, rocks, small plastic toys, etc.)

Just like those dried berries in the cereal box, larger objects in an avalanche will tend to drift to the top of the heap. You can do this project to see how this works.

1 Put your objects into the jar and fill the jar almost to the top with rice.

2 Put the lid on the jar.

3 Shake the jar, and see how long it takes for different objects to move to the surface. Did one size float up faster than another? Is there a particular shape that seems to move faster to the surface? What about small shapes—do they rise quickly or remain hidden in the rice?

DID YOU KNOW?

Within five seconds of starting, an avalanche can move at 80 miles per hour (129 kilometers per hour)!

101

CHAPTER NINE
UNUSUAL EVENTS

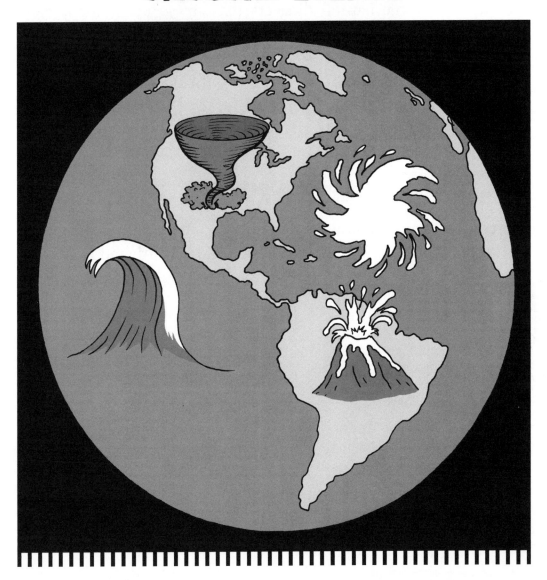

You're probably familiar with most of the natural disasters you've read about so far. And it's possible that you've even experienced one or more of them. Lots of people have felt an earthquake rumble or watched the snow from inside during a blizzard. Maybe you've experienced the power of a hurricane or seen the damage from a tornado.

But there are some natural disasters that are so uncommon, most people have never heard of them at all.

THESE UNUSUAL EVENTS AREN'T LIKELY TO HAPPEN IN YOUR NEIGHBORHOOD AND MAY NEVER EVEN HAPPEN AGAIN ON THE WHOLE PLANET!

LIMNIC ERUPTION

Most of the time, a natural disaster involves a lot of noise, disruption, and force. There's usually extreme chaos and a whirlwind of activity that goes along with it.

WORDS TO KNOW

LIMNIC ERUPTION: an eruption of gas that occurs when a high amount of carbon dioxide bursts out of a lake.

STEALTHY: silent or secret movement.

In a normal volcanic eruption, there are lava fountains and massive explosions. But in a **LIMNIC ERUPTION**, there's no smoke, fire, ash, or lava. Limnic eruptions are **STEALTHY**, and very deadly. There have only been two limnic eruptions in history, and both happened at lakes in the West African country of Cameroon.

DID YOU KNOW?

In 1984 at Lake Monoun, the first-ever limnic eruption killed 37 people. Two years later at Lake Nyos, over 1,700 people died in a second, larger limnic eruption.

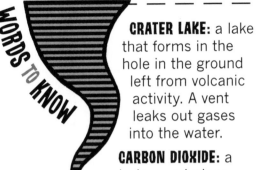

CRATER LAKE: a lake that forms in the hole in the ground left from volcanic activity. A vent leaks out gases into the water.

CARBON DIOXIDE: a colorless, odorless gas. It forms when animals breathe and when plants and other living matter die and rot.

SUFFOCATE: to kill or destroy by cutting off access to air or oxygen.

In **CRATER LAKES** like these, it is not unusual for a large bubble of **CARBON DIOXIDE** to get trapped at the bottom. Since carbon dioxide is denser than air, it normally doesn't rise to the surface. But at Lake Monoun and later at Lake Nyos, the gas bubble rose to the top and suddenly erupted in the lake, bursting out of the water and into the air.

THE ENORMOUS AMOUNT OF GAS THAT IT RELEASED **SUFFOCATED** EVERYTHING IN ITS PATH.

Gas blew out of Lake Nyos at 60 miles per hour (97 kilometers per hour) and went racing through the surrounding landscape at about 30 miles an hour (48 kilometers per hour). Because of its speed, the gas pushed away all the oxygen in the nearby villages, and the residents and animals were left with no air to breathe.

WHY CAMEROON?

A limnic eruption is incredibly rare because conditions have to be absolutely perfect for one to happen. In Cameroon, they've had two! But why did the bubbles burst?

- First, these lakes are very deep, and they're lakes formed from volcanoes that continue to release gas.

- Second, the lakes were completely saturated with carbon dioxide. That means they had so much of the gas in them that it didn't have anywhere else to go.

All the gas in these lakes made them very unstable and it just took one "trigger" to set them off. Imagine the bubbles building up so much pressure in a soda bottle until it can't hold any more bubbles. What would happen if you shook the bottle? A huge explosion of sticky, sugary soda all over you! Well, an earthquake can shake the bubbles in a lake in the same way. On the day of the Lake Monoun eruption, there were reports of a nearby earthquake. That could be what burst the bubble that day. At Lake Nyos, scientists think landslides set off the eruption. ◉

DID YOU KNOW?

Scientists are keeping an eye on Lake Kivu, also in Africa, to prevent a limnic eruption there. Lake Kivu is 2,000 times bigger than Lake Nyos. More than 2 million people live on its shores.

To prevent any more of these disasters, scientists are trying to safely remove the carbon dioxide from the lakes. The process is actually simple. By sticking a long pipe into the lake, they can move the gas from the bottom of the lake into the air at a slow, safe rate.

WORDS TO KNOW

SUCTION: to remove or draw away by using a force, such as a pump, to create a difference in pressure. It makes a fluid flow from an area of higher pressure to an area of lower pressure.

With just a little bit of pumping, the water from the bottom of the lake is drawn up the pipe. It doesn't take long for the water pressure to drop and the gas bubbles to release. This sends a huge spray of water out the top of the pipe. As the water rises, it creates **SUCTION** at the bottom of the pipe, so the water just keeps shooting out!

CARBON DIOXIDE GAS ACCUMULATION

THE PROBLEM IS THAT THERE IS SO MUCH CARBON DIOXIDE IN THE LAKES. SCIENTISTS AREN'T SURE THESE SIMPLE PIPES WILL REALLY REMOVE ENOUGH GAS IN EACH OF THE LAKES TO MAKE THEM SAFE.

TUNGUSKA EVENT

Compared to the relatively quiet events of the limnic eruptions, what happened in 1908 in Russia came with a bang! At around 7 a.m. on June 30, an enormous explosion rocked an area in western Siberia. Witnesses reported seeing a brilliant moving light just before the explosion. The shock wave that followed knocked people right off their feet and broke windows miles away.

Was it an earthquake? No, although the explosion was equivalent to a 5.0 earthquake on the Richter scale. And it wasn't a volcanic eruption, either.

WORDS TO KNOW

METEOROID: a rock that orbits the sun. It is smaller than an asteroid and at least as large as a speck of dust. It becomes a meteor when it enters Earth's atmosphere and a meteorite when it lands on the earth.

COMET: a ball of ice and dust that orbits the sun.

Scientists believe that the explosion was caused by a large **METEOROID** or piece of a **COMET** that burst several miles above the earth's surface. Thankfully, very few people lived in the area of the explosion that let out a thousand times more energy than an atomic bomb.

About 80 million trees were toppled by the blast. It would have destroyed a city. The Tunguska event was the largest space-related event to impact the earth in recorded history.

MEGA DISASTERS

For every natural disaster, there are scientists and others who believe there could be a "mega" version—a natural disaster so large it boggles the mind, like a mega volcano that would wipe out half a continent.

In 1958, a mega tsunami really did happen. In Lituya Bay, Alaska, a major earthquake split 90 million tons of rock and ice off the mountainside all at once. The rock and ice landed like the world's biggest cannonball in the bay's deep water.

The result was the highest wave ever recorded, an amazing 1,720 feet high (524 meters). That's taller than all but five of the tallest skyscrapers on the planet. This mega tsunami would have knocked any one of those buildings right over.

The mega tsunami was a frightening example of what any natural disaster, extremely magnified, could do.

FORTUNATELY, WITH THE EXCEPTION OF THIS MEGA TSUNAMI, OTHER MEGA DISASTERS HAVE NOT HAPPENED IN RECORDED HISTORY, WHICH IS A VERY, VERY LONG TIME.

MAKE YOUR OWN
LAKE ERUPTION

SUPPLIES
* two, 2-liter bottles of soda
* table or other stable surface
* 2 packs of Mentos candy, mint flavored
* skateboard
* cardboard
* duct tape
* pavement or concrete surface

This experiment will help you see just how powerful a force carbon dioxide gas can be in a liquid. Gather everyone who wants to watch this easy and quick project! Be sure to do this experiment outdoors, away from anything that shouldn't get messy or wet. And have an adult on hand to supervise.

1 Open one soda bottle and set it on a stable surface.

2 Unwrap one end of the candy roll. Gently squish the candy inside the wrapper to loosen the pieces up. As quickly as you can, slide all the candies into the soda bottle, stand back and watch what happens when the candy reacts with the soda!

3 Now use the soda and candy to power a rocket car! Get a skateboard and place it on a hard, flat surface like pavement or concrete. If it's curved at the ends, use cardboard to make the body of the board level. Then, use duct tape to strap the soda bottle on its side to the board. You want the neck of the bottle to hang over the end of the board.

4 Holding the board upright, so the bottle opening faces up, take off the cap and drop in the candy. As fast as you can, put the skateboard back on the smooth, hard surface. The force of the eruption will launch the skateboard across the concrete!

MAKE YOUR OWN
CRATER EXPERIMENT

SUPPLIES

* 2 aluminum pans or cookie sheets with edges

* flour

* plaster of Paris or clay

What would happen if a meteor hit the earth? Would it matter how big it was, or how fast it was falling? Try this experiment to find out.

1 Pour an inch or two of flour into each pan (2½ to 5 centimeters). Shake the pan to distribute the flour evenly.

2 Mix up the plaster of Paris according to the directions or soften your clay. Use it to make several meteors. Make some the same size and others of different sizes. If you're using plaster of Paris, wait until your meteors dry and harden. If you're using clay, you can use them right away.

3 Drop different-sized meteors into the flour from the same height. Then try dropping same-sized meteors at different speeds. First drop them gently, then throw them with a little more force. Remove the meteors carefully each time so you don't change their size.

4 Take a look at the craters left behind. Did the size of the meteor make a difference in the crater? How about the speed of the meteor?

CHAPTER TEN
THE IMPACT OF NATURAL DISASTERS

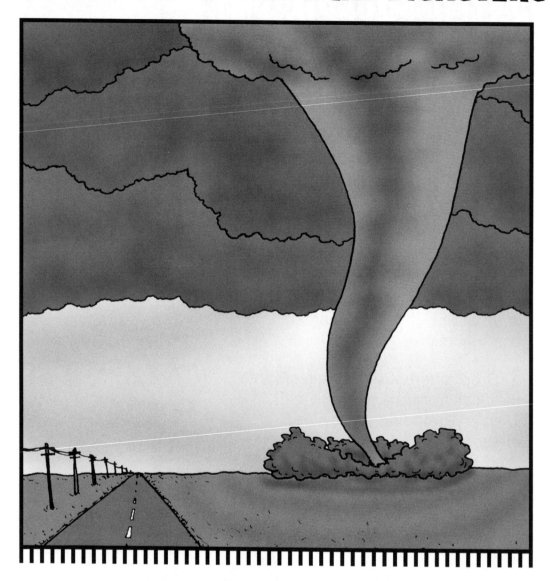

Picture a volcano erupting in an area where no one lived for hundreds of miles. Or imagine a tornado tearing across empty land and then breaking up harmlessly. If natural disasters happened like that, it would save thousands of lives.

But unfortunately, many people live in the shadow of live volcanoes or close to riverbanks within a flood zone. There's no place that's free from the chance of any disaster—whether it's wildfires in dry, hot areas or blizzards in cold places.

Natural disasters have a strong impact on everyday life. Normal routines can be disrupted for days, weeks, or even much longer. Rebuilding takes time and money. And it can take a while for things like electricity or roads to be restored.

NATURAL DISASTERS OF THE PAST HAD THE POTENTIAL TO HARM MANY PEOPLE BECAUSE WARNING SYSTEMS WERE SO POOR. TODAY THERE IS A DIFFERENT PROBLEM. WE HAVE BETTER WAYS TO WATCH FOR POTENTIAL DISASTERS, BUT THE POPULATION OF THE PLANET HAS GROWN.

That means there are more people that live in harm's way. People choose to live next to volcanoes or along rivers because of fertile land or scenic views.

Fortunately, today's scientists have many ways to monitor potential natural disasters. And there are a lot of ways to spread the information if they need to send out a warning—on television, by telephone, on the radio, or over the Internet. Although there are areas that are still "off the grid" and don't receive these communications, scientists are working on advanced notice systems to help reduce the chance of anyone getting hurt.

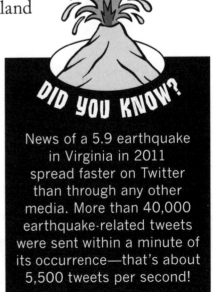

DID YOU KNOW?

News of a 5.9 earthquake in Virginia in 2011 spread faster on Twitter than through any other media. More than 40,000 earthquake-related tweets were sent within a minute of its occurrence—that's about 5,500 tweets per second!

GLOBAL NEIGHBORHOOD

With the way information is shared globally, people all over the world can quickly find out about a major disaster that has happened in a distant land. And every time there's a big disaster, people far and wide jump to help those in need. Whether they're offering money to help rebuild an area, volunteering time and skills to physically help the rebuilding process, or donating food and clothing to help with immediate needs, people around the world rally together to help those who have experienced something disastrous. It's inspiring how much neighbors, friends, and even people and governments from distant countries reach out to help others in tough times.

There are even web sites, such as NationMaster.com, to see how much assistance countries from around the world have contributed to specific natural disasters. This site includes statistics for several recent disasters, including the 2004 Indian Ocean tsunami, Hurricane Katrina, the 2010 earthquake in Haiti, and the 2011 tsunami that struck Japan. ◉

MAKE YOUR OWN
HOME EMERGENCY KIT

SUPPLIES

* large, waterproof duffle bag or plastic bin
* recommended supplies (list below)
* paper
* pen

For any natural disaster, you'll be one step ahead if you have a home emergency kit assembled and ready to go. You never know when something is going to happen— that's what makes natural disasters so scary. But if you've got your kit together, you can at least feel comfortable knowing you're prepared to handle what comes your way.

1 You'll need the same gear for most types of emergencies. Put the items from this list into your bag or bin, then think about what your own family needs and add those items, too.

* Water jugs
* Canned food
* Can opener
* Flashlights and batteries
* Any medication family members need
* Blankets
* Matches
* First aid kit
* Hand wipes or sanitizer
* Basic tool set
* Battery-powered radio

2 On the paper, write down a list of what's in your kit. Every now and then, check the dates on the food and replace what's getting old.

3 Be sure to keep your kit in a location where you'll be able to find it quickly and easily in case of an emergency. You'll want it if the power's out or if your home is damaged.

MAKE YOUR OWN
PET EMERGENCY KIT

Don't forget about your pets during an emergency! If you have to evacuate your house, bring your pets with you if you can. You might not be able to get back to your house soon, and you want to be sure they're safe.

1 Just like with the kit for people, stock your pet emergency kit with things your pet will need in an emergency.

- Food
- Identification
- Photo in case your pet is lost
- Leash or carrier
- Your vet's phone number
- Light pet dishes
- Rope
- Water
- Blanket

Buddy's Emergency Kit

ABSORB: to soak up.

ACTIVE VOLCANO: a volcano that has erupted in recent recorded time.

AIR PRESSURE: the weight, or force, of the atmosphere in a place.

ALTITUDE: the height of something above the level of the sea. Also called elevation.

ARCHAEOLOGIST: a scientist who studies ancient people through the objects they left behind.

ARSONIST: someone who deliberately sets a fire to property that doesn't belong to them.

ATMOSPHERE: the gases surrounding the earth.

BEACON: a device that sends out a signal, indicating location.

CARBON DIOXIDE: a colorless, odorless gas. It forms when animals breathe and when plants and other living matter die and rot.

CATASTROPHIC: extremely harmful or damaging.

CATEGORY: the word used to classify the strength of hurricanes, from one to five.

CE: put after a date, CE stands for Common Era and counts up from zero. BCE stands for Before the Common Era and counts down to zero. These are non-religious terms that correspond to AD and BC.

CIVILIZATION: a community of people that is advanced in art, science, and government.

CLOCKWISE: in the same direction as the hands of a clock move.

COMET: a ball of ice and dust that orbits the sun.

CONVECTION: movement from one place to another caused by the heating up of molecules, such as when warm air rises.

COUNTERCLOCKWISE: in the opposite direction to the way the hands of a clock move.

CRATER LAKE: a lake that forms in the hole in the ground left from volcanic activity. A vent leaks out gases into the water.

CROP: a plant grown for food and other uses.

CRUST: the outer surface of the earth.

CYCLONE: the name of a hurricane over the Indian Ocean, the Bay of Bengal, and Australia.

DAM: a barrier constructed across a waterway to control the flow or raise the level of water.

DENSE: tightly packed together.

DESALINATE: to remove the salt from salt water.

DORMANT VOLCANO: a volcano that is still capable of erupting, but hasn't for a long time.

DROUGHT: a long period of unusually low rainfall that can harm plants and animals.

EARTHQUAKE: when pieces of the outer layer of the earth suddenly move.

EL NIÑO: warming of the ocean surface off the western coast of South America that occurs every 4 to 12 years. It creates unusual weather patterns in different parts of the world.

EPICENTER: the point on the earth's crust where an earthquake starts.

EQUATOR: the imaginary line around the earth halfway between the North and South Poles.

GLOSSARY

EROSION: when land is worn away by wind or water.

ERUPT: to burst suddenly.

EVAPORATE: when a liquid heats up and changes into a gas, or vapor.

EVOLVE: to change or develop slowly, over time.

EXCAVATE: to dig out material from the ground.

EXTINCT VOLCANO: a volcano that doesn't have any magma flow anymore, so it won't erupt again.

EYE: the center of the hurricane where winds are swirling in both directions.

FAMINE: a severe shortage of food.

FAULT: a place on the earth's crust that's weak and likely to be the spot of an earthquake.

FERTILE: land that is rich in nutrients and good for growing crops.

FIRE-RESISTANT: difficult to burn.

FIRE TOLERANT: able to survive being burned in a fire.

FLAMMABLE: something that easily catches on fire.

FLASH FLOOD: a sudden rush of water onto an area of land that is normally dry.

FRONT: the dividing point where two types of air meet.

FROSTBITE: damage that can happen to your exposed skin when you're out in freezing temperatures.

GULF COAST: the states that are on the Gulf of Mexico, which include Texas, Louisiana, Mississippi, Alabama, and Florida.

HABITAT: the natural area where a plant or animal lives.

HEAT INDEX: how hot it feels when you combine air temperature with humidity.

HEAT STROKE: a dangerous condition that's caused when someone overheats because of high temperatures.

HUMID: a high level of moisture in the air.

HYDROELECTRIC: generating electricity by water power.

INFERNO: a large fire that is dangerously out of control.

INNER CORE: the very middle of the earth.

IRRIGATE: to supply land with water, usually for crops.

LAVA: hot, melted rock that has risen to the surface of the earth.

LEVEE: a wall, usually made of earth, that is built to hold back water.

LIMNIC ERUPTION: an eruption of gas that occurs when a high amount of carbon dioxide bursts out of a lake.

LIVESTOCK: animals kept by people to do work or for food.

MAGMA: partially melted rock below the surface of the earth.

MAGNITUDE: the measurement of the strength of an earthquake.

MANTLE: the layer of the earth around the core.

METEORITE: a piece of rock that falls from space and lands on Earth's surface.

METEOROID: a rock that orbits the sun. It is smaller than an asteroid and at least as large as a speck of dust. It becomes a meteor when it enters Earth's atmosphere and a meteorite when it lands on the earth.

METEOROLOGIST: someone who studies weather and makes predictions about it.

MICROORGANISM: a life form that is so small it takes a microscope to see it.

MINERALS: nutrients found in rocks and soil that keep plants and animals healthy and growing.

MOLECULES: tiny particles that make up objects.

MOLTEN: melted by heat to form a liquid.

MULTIPLE-VORTEX VOLCANO: a tornado with several different funnels reaching down from the main storm system.

NILE DELTA: a fan-shaped area of land in northeastern Egypt at the mouth of the Nile River where it empties into the Mediterranean Sea.

NUTRIENTS: substances that living things need to live and grow.

OUTER CORE: the layer of the earth between the inner core and the mantle.

OXYGEN: a gas in the air that people and animals need to breathe to stay alive.

PLATES: large sections of the earth's crust.

POINT OF ORIGIN: the location where an earthquake begins.

PRECIPITATION: the water that falls to the ground in the form of rain, snow, hail, mist, or sleet.

RADAR: a device that detects objects by bouncing radio waves off them and measuring how long it takes for the waves to return.

RADIATION: energy that comes from a source and travels through something, like the radiation from an X-ray that travels through a person.

RESERVOIR: a manmade or natural lake used to collect water that can be stored for future use.

SATELLITE: a device that orbits the earth to relay communication signals or transmit information.

SATURATED: full of moisture.

SEISMIC WAVES: the energy that travels outward from the epicenter of an earthquake.

SEISMOGRAPH: an instrument that measures the movement of the earth's crust.

SLOPE: the slant of a mountain.

SMOLDERING: when a fire is burning very slowly, possibly without any visible flames coming up.

SNOWDRIFT: a bank of deep snow heaped up by the wind.

SOOT: the fine black powder left behind when coal, wood, oil, or other fuels burn.

STEALTHY: silent or secret movement.

STORM SURGE: the sea water pushed along by a hurricane. It rushes inland and causes flooding when the storm reaches the coastline.

SUCTION: to remove or draw away by using a force, such as a pump, to create a difference in pressure. It makes a fluid flow from an area of higher pressure to an area of lower pressure.

SUFFOCATE: to kill or destroy by cutting off access to air or oxygen.

SUPERCELL: a severe thunderstorm with strong movements of air both up and down.

TNT: short for trinitrotoluene. A poisonous chemical mixture used as an explosive.

GLOSSARY

TORNADO OUTBREAK: a series of tornadoes that come from the same storm system.

TORRENT: a violently fast stream of water.

TROPICAL CYCLONE: any low-pressure system with swirling winds that starts over tropical or subtropical waters.

TSUNAMI: an enormous wave formed by a disturbance under the water, like an earthquake or volcano.

TYPHOON: the name of a hurricane over the western Pacific Ocean.

UNDERBRUSH: shrubs and small trees that grow beneath the taller trees in a forest.

UNSTABLE: when temperatures drop very quickly with height, or when a layer of dry air sits over moist surface air.

VISIBILITY: the distance we can see in the light and weather conditions.

VOLCANO: an opening in the earth's surface through which lava, ash, and gases can burst out.

VOLCANOLOGIST: a scientist who studies volcanoes.

VOLUME: the amount of space taken up by water or anything else that is three dimensional.

WATER VAPOR: the gas form of water in the air.

WHITEOUT: the condition in blizzards where you can't see anything because of blowing snow.

WILDFIRE: a large, destructive fire that spreads out of control.

WIND CHILL: the temperature it feels like when you combine the air temperature with the wind speed.

RESOURCES

BOOKS

Griffey, Harriet. *DK Readers: Earthquakes and Other Natural Disasters.* DK, 2010.

Guiberson, Brenda Z. *Disasters: Natural and Man-Made Catastrophes Through the Centuries.* Henry Holt, 2010.

Mason, Paul. *The World's Most Dangerous Places.* Heinemann-Raintree, 2007.

Tarshis, Lauren. *I Survived Hurricane Katrina.* Scholastic, 2011.

WEB SITES

earthquake.usgs.gov

www.fema.gov/kids

www.state.nj.us/drbc/drought/kids_droughtinfo.htm

www.smokeybear.com

INDEX